An Analysis of

Richard H. Thaler and Cass R. Sunstein's

Nudge
Improving Decisions about Health, Wealth, and Happiness

Mark Egan

www.macat.com
info@macat.com

Cover illustration: Etienne Gilfillan

Cataloguing in Publication Data
A catalogue record for this book is available from the British Library.
Library of Congress Cataloguing-in-Publication Data is available upon request.

ISBN 978-1-912303-67-0 (hardback)
ISBN 978-1-912128-03-7 (paperback)
ISBN 978-1-912282-55-5 (e-book)

CONTENTS

THE MACAT LIBRARY

The Macat Library is a series of unique academic explorations of seminal works in the humanities and social sciences – books and papers that have had a significant and widely recognised impact on their disciplines. It has been created to serve as much more than just a summary of what lies between the covers of a great book. It illuminates and explores the influences on, ideas of, and impact of that book. Our goal is to offer a learning resource that encourages critical thinking and fosters a better, deeper understanding of important ideas.

Each publication is divided into three Sections: Influences, Ideas, and Impact. Each Section has four Modules. These explore every important facet of the work, and the responses to it.

This Section-Module structure makes a Macat Library book easy to use, but it has another important feature. Because each Macat book is written to the same format, it is possible (and encouraged!) to cross-reference multiple Macat books along the same lines of inquiry or research. This allows the reader to open up interesting interdisciplinary pathways.

To further aid your reading, lists of glossary terms and people mentioned are included at the end of this book (these are indicated by an asterisk [*] throughout) – as well as a list of works cited.

Macat has worked with the University of Cambridge to identify the elements of critical thinking and understand the ways in which six different skills combine to enable effective thinking.
Three allow us to fully understand a problem; three more give us the tools to solve it. Together, these six skills make up the **PACIER** model of critical thinking. They are:

ANALYSIS – understanding how an argument is built
EVALUATION – exploring the strengths and weaknesses of an argument
INTERPRETATION – understanding issues of meaning

CREATIVE THINKING – coming up with new ideas and fresh connections
PROBLEM-SOLVING – producing strong solutions
REASONING – creating strong arguments

To find out more, visit **WWW.MACAT.COM.**

CRITICAL THINKING AND *NUDGE*

Primary critical thinking skill: REASONING
Secondary critical thinking skill: CREATIVE THINKING

When it was published in 2008, Richard Thaler and Cass Sunstein's *Nudge: Improving Decisions about Health, Wealth, and Happiness* quickly became one of the most influential books in modern economics and politics. Within a short time, it had inspired whole government departments in the US and UK, and others as far afield as Singapore.

One of the keys to *Nudge*'s success is Thaler and Sunstein's ability to create a detailed and persuasive case for their take on economic decision-making. *Nudge* is not a book packed with original findings or data; instead it is a careful and systematic synthesis of decades of research into behavioral economics. The discipline challenges much conventional economic thought – which works on the basis that, overall, humans make rational decisions – by focusing instead on the 'irrational' cognitive biases that affect our decision making. These seemingly in-built biases mean that certain kinds of economic decision-making are predictably irrational.

Thaler and Sunstein prove themselves experts at creating persuasive arguments and dealing effectively with counter-arguments. They conclude that if governments understand these cognitive biases, they can 'nudge' us into making better decisions for ourselves. Entertaining as well as smart, Nudge shows the full range of reasoning skills that go into making a persuasive argument.

ABOUT THE AUTHORS OF THE ORIGINAL WORK

US economist **Richard H. Thaler** (b. 1945) is credited with being a founding father of the field of behavioral economics and has been tipped as a future Nobel Prize winner. His colleague, the legal scholar **Cass R. Sunstein** (b. 1954), served in the administration of Barack Obama from 2009 to 2012 and is one of the most frequently cited legal scholars in the world today. Both men taught at the University of Chicago and collaborated on their influential 2008 book *Nudge: Improving Decisions about Health, Wealth, and Happiness*, which argued that governments can help people make better decisions, while still respecting their freedom of choice. It was named one of the best books of 2008 by respected magazine *The Economist*.

ABOUT THE AUTHOR OF THE ANALYSIS

Mark Egan is a doctoral candidate in behavioural science at the University of Stirling Management School. He holds an MSc in human decision science from Maastricht University and, in addition to his doctoral research, works with the Behavioural Insights Team advising the UK government on behavioural science and policy decisions.

ABOUT MACAT

GREAT WORKS FOR CRITICAL THINKING

Macat is focused on making the ideas of the world's great thinkers accessible and comprehensible to everybody, everywhere, in ways that promote the development of enhanced critical thinking skills.

It works with leading academics from the world's top universities to produce new analyses that focus on the ideas and the impact of the most influential works ever written across a wide variety of academic disciplines. Each of the works that sit at the heart of its growing library is an enduring example of great thinking. But by setting them in context – and looking at the influences that shaped their authors, as well as the responses they provoked – Macat encourages readers to look at these classics and game-changers with fresh eyes. Readers learn to think, engage and challenge their ideas, rather than simply accepting them.

'Macat offers an amazing first-of-its-kind tool for interdisciplinary learning and research. Its focus on works that transformed their disciplines and its rigorous approach, drawing on the world's leading experts and educational institutions, opens up a world-class education to anyone.'

Andreas Schleicher
Director for Education and Skills, Organisation for Economic Co-operation and Development

'Macat is taking on some of the major challenges in university education … They have drawn together a strong team of active academics who are producing teaching materials that are novel in the breadth of their approach.'

Prof Lord Broers,
former Vice-Chancellor of the University of Cambridge

'The Macat vision is exceptionally exciting. It focuses upon new modes of learning which analyse and explain seminal texts which have profoundly influenced world thinking and so social and economic development. It promotes the kind of critical thinking which is essential for any society and economy.
This is the learning of the future.'

Rt Hon Charles Clarke, former UK Secretary of State for Education

'The Macat analyses provide immediate access to the critical conversation surrounding the books that have shaped their respective discipline, which will make them an invaluable resource to all of those, students and teachers, working in the field.'

Professor William Tronzo, University of California at San Diego

WAYS IN TO THE TEXT

KEY POINTS

- The economist Richard Thaler and legal scholar Cass Sunstein are prominent American academics who worked together at the University of Chicago in the 1990s and the 2000s.

- In *Nudge: Improving Decisions about Health, Wealth, and Happiness*, Thaler and Sunstein introduced "libertarian paternalism,"* "choice architecture,"* and "nudging"* as tools for governments to help people make better decisions while respecting their freedom of choice.

- *Nudge* has influenced policy-making in the United Kingdom, United States, and several other countries. It is one of the most influential public policy books in recent years.

Who Are Richard Thaler and Cass Sunstein?

Richard H. Thaler, coauthor of *Nudge: Improving Decisions about Health, Wealth, and Happiness* (2008), was born in 1945. He completed his PhD in Economics at the University of Rochester in 1974 and has worked at the University of Chicago since 1995. Early in his career, Thaler was introduced to the work of the Israeli psychologists Daniel Kahneman* and Amos Tversky,* who would become important influences. Thaler became professor of behavioral science and economics at the Chicago Booth School of Business and established himself as a founding figure in the field of behavioral economics* (a subdiscipline of the field of economics which draws on findings from the discipline of psychology to formulate models of economic decision-making). Many academics consider Thaler a likely future winner of the Nobel Prize in Economics.[1]

Cass R. Sunstein was born in 1954 and graduated from Harvard Law School in 1978. He worked at the University of Chicago from 1981 to 2008. During that time he wrote several articles applying behavioral economics to law and in total has published over 500 articles on a diverse set of topics. From 2009 to 2012 he served in the Obama Administration.* Currently the Robert Walmsley University Professor at Harvard, Sunstein is one of the most cited legal scholars in the world today.

In the 1990s, Thaler and Sunstein began to write *Nudge* at the University of Chicago, considered by many academics to be the home of the Chicago school*—an approach to economic theory known as neoclassical economics.* According to neoclassical economic theory, people make rational economic decisions on the basis of complete information. While, for the most part, *Nudge* strongly disagrees with this assumption, Thaler and Sunstein did not reject all the ideas of the Chicago school; their work builds on the influential Chicago economist Milton Friedman's* idea that people should be "free to choose."[2]

What Does *Nudge* Say?

In *Nudge*, Thaler and Sunstein argue that governments can help people make better decisions while respecting their freedom of choice.

Governments can do this by creating better "choice architecture." A choice architect designs the environment in which people make decisions. A simple example is a cafeteria manager who encourages healthy eating by placing vegetables first in a line of food options. Changing the choice architecture like this to encourage a certain behavior is what Thaler and Sunstein call a "nudge." Other examples of a nudge might be a driver's satellite navigation system, a sign that encourages people to take the stairs instead of the elevator, or government nutritional guidelines. These things encourage people to behave in a certain way, but do not force them to do so.

Thaler and Sunstein argue that governments should nudge people to make better decisions. However, people themselves must judge these decisions as "better," not the government. Thaler and Sunstein call their philosophy "libertarian paternalism."

This may seem a contradiction: libertarianism* is a political philosophy that emphasizes individual freedom and opposes government intervention, while paternalism* means to act on a person's behalf for what is deemed to be their own good. But Thaler and Sunstein reconcile this contradiction through a subtle argument. They say that interventions are permissible provided they do not restrict freedom of choice, giving the example of a firm that wants its workers to save more.[3] The firm nudges them to do so by enrolling them in a pension plan, but if the employees wish to opt out, they can do so. The general tendency of people to stick with a default option causes the savings rate to increase. This nudge also preserves freedom of choice because employees can choose not to use the plan.

Thaler and Sunstein argue that nudges can have significant and predictable effects, rejecting the assumptions underlying the main economic theories of human behavior. Many economists assume a model of behavior in which people are perfectly informed, have infinite cognitive ability, and unlimited self-control. Nudges cannot affect these "rational actors."* *Nudge* argues that real people have natural limitations in knowledge, cognitive ability, and self-control. Cognitive biases* (ways of interpreting the world that lead people away from rational judgments and behavior) and social pressures influence their decisions. Nudges can affect them.

Thaler and Sunstein call these groups "Econs"* (ideal decision-makers in economic models) and "Humans" (people who make decisions in the real world), and maintain that nudges can help

11

Humans make better decisions. To support their argument, they cite decades of research in psychology and behavioral economics, showing how psychological factors can cause people to make poor decisions.

Thaler and Sunstein positioned their policies as a "real third way"[*4] for American politics. They hoped nudging could appeal both to Democrats,[*] traditionally supportive of government intervention, and Republicans,[*] traditionally opposed to it.

Why Does *Nudge* Matter?

Nudge is one of the most influential books on public policy published in recent years. Its ideas are relevant to public policy, academic research, and private business. It has made its mark in all three fields.

In the United Kingdom, the right-wing Conservative party[*] embraced the book's ideas almost immediately after publication. In 2010, Prime Minister David Cameron[*] created the world's first governmental "Nudge Unit"[*] (officially called the Behavioural Insights Team). That group's success inspired the creation of the American Social and Behavioral Sciences Team[*] in 2015. *Nudge* has also influenced civil servants in Germany, the Netherlands, Finland, Singapore, and Australia.[5]

Nudge has stimulated a great deal of interest in the academic world. It has received over 5,000 citations from economics, psychology, public health, marketing, sociology, medicine, political science, criminology, philosophy, and other disciplines.[6] Many of these disciplines have adapted the book's ideas to new contexts and problems.

The ideas of *Nudge* also apply to the business world. A 2008 article in the *Harvard Business Review* describes how businesses can nudge their customers to buy their products.[7] A 2014 article in *Forbes* describes the way behavioral economics has affected the advertising industry as a whole.[8] Google has applied the book's ideas by using nudges in their company cafeteria.[9]

Thaler and Sunstein have continued to promote *Nudge* since its publication. Thaler has advised the Nudge Unit on tax collection and energy efficiency.[10] Sunstein applied the book's ideas as administrator of the Office of Information and Regulatory Affairs from 2009 to 2012. Both have engaged with the book's critics through interviews, articles, and books.

Nudge remains essential reading for anyone interested in the science of behavior change.

NOTES

1 Noah Smith, "Five Economists Who Deserve Nobels," *Bloomberg View*, December 9, 2014, accessed September 4, 2015, http:/www.bloombergview.com/articles/2014-12–09/five-economists-who-deserve-nobels.

2 Richard H. Thaler and Cass R. Sunstein, *Nudge: Improving Decisions about Health, Wealth, and Happiness* (New York: Yale University Press, 2008), 5.

3 Thaler and Sunstein, *Nudge*, 109.

4 Thaler and Sunstein, *Nudge*, 252.

5 Behavioural Insights Team, "The Behavioural Insights Team Update Report 2013–2015," accessed September 4, 2015, http:/www.behaviouralinsights.co.uk/wp-content/uploads/2015/07/BIT_Update-Report-Final-2013–2015.pdf.

6 Google Scholar records 5,495 texts which have cited *Nudge* as of September 26, 2015: https://scholar.google.com/scholar?cites=16854468477297806637&as_sdt=2005&sciodt=0,5&hl=en.

7 Daniel G. Goldstein et al., "Nudge Your Customers toward Better Choices," *Harvard Business Review*, December 2008, accessed September 4, 2015, https://hbr.org/2008/12/nudge-your-customers-toward-better-choices.

8 John Orwid, "Behavioral Economics Gives the Advertising Industry a Nudge in the Right Direction," *Forbes*, February 5, 2014, accessed September 26, 2015, http:/www.forbes.com/sites/johnowrid/2014/02/05/behavioural-economics-gives-the-advertising-industry-a-nudge-in-the-right-direction/.

9 Cliff Kuang, "In the Cafeteria, Google Gets Healthy," *Fast Company Magazine*, March 19, 2012, accessed September 4, 2015, http:/www.fastcompany.com/1822516/cafeteria-google-gets-healthy.

10 Douglas Clement, "Interview with Richard Thaler," The Region Magazine, October 3, 2013, accessed September 4, 2015, https://www.minneapolisfed.org/publications/the-region/interview-with-richard-thaler.

SECTION 1
INFLUENCES

MODULE 1
THE AUTHORS AND THE HISTORICAL CONTEXT

KEY POINTS

- *Nudge* is one of the most significant books on public policy published in recent years.

- Its authors were influenced by studies in psychology about human decision-making, particularly work by the Israeli psychologists Daniel Kahneman* and Amos Tversky.*

- In *Nudge*, Thaler and Sunstein use theories from behavioral economics* to argue that governments should help their citizens to make better decisions while respecting their freedom of choice.

Why Read This Text?

In 2008, Richard H. Thaler, professor of behavioral science and economics at the University of Chicago, and Cass R. Sunstein, then professor of jurisprudence at the University of Chicago, published *Nudge: Improving Decisions about Health, Wealth, and Happiness.*

Their main argument in *Nudge* is that governments can help people make better decisions while respecting their freedom of choice. This can be achieved by organizing the environment in which people make decisions—what Thaler and Sunstein call choice architecture*—for example, the cafeteria that promotes healthy eating by putting fruits first and desserts last. Other examples might be a firm that automatically enrolls its employees into a retirement savings program while allowing them to opt out, or a website that recommends products based on your past purchases. These examples all encourage certain behaviors without banning any options or

> ❝ Yes, there is such a thing as common sense ... That's this reader's reaction to Richard Thaler and Cass Sunstein's 'Nudge,' an engaging and insightful tour through the evidence that most human beings don't make decisions [as they do] in elementary economics textbooks, along with a rich array of suggestions for enabling many of us to make better choices, both for ourselves and for society. ❞
>
> Benjamin M. Friedman, "Guiding Forces," *New York Times*

forcing any particular choice. Thaler and Sunstein call these kinds of interventions "nudges."*

In the seven years since its publication, *Nudge* has received over 5,000 citations and influenced a diverse set of academic disciplines.[1] It has directly influenced policy-making at the highest levels of government in the United Kingdom and United States. It has influenced firms in marketing, consulting, management, and many other industries. *Nudge* remains essential reading for anyone interested in the science of decision-making and behavior change.

Authors' Lives

Richard H. Thaler received his PhD in economics in 1974. Although he was taught economic theories that assumed perfectly rational models of human decision-making, early in his career Thaler was influenced by the Israeli psychologists Daniel Kahneman and Amos Tversky, whose work contradicted these assumptions about human rationality. Thaler later integrated their insights (and other work from psychology) into economics to become a founding figure in the new field of behavioral economics. *Nudge* was based on theories from this field.

Cass R. Sunstein graduated with a JD from Harvard Law School in 1975. He has written prolifically throughout his career, including several influential texts applying the ideas of behavioral economics to law. Sunstein is also a noted proponent of judicial minimalism,* a legal philosophy that argues for small, case-specific interpretations of constitutional law* (those laws enshrined in a country's constitution). This philosophy may be indicative of Sunstein's preference for the incremental, "soft," interventions discussed in *Nudge*.

Thaler and Sunstein wrote *Nudge* during their shared tenure at the University of Chicago during the 1990s and 2000s. Ironically, the Chicago school* is considered the home of traditional neoclassical economics,* which *Nudge* rebelled against—particularly its assumption that people make economic decisions with perfect rationality. The authors did not, however, entirely reject the ideas of the Chicago school: the concept of nudging builds on the Chicago economist Milton Friedman's* idea that people should be "free to choose."[2]

Authors' Background

In the opening chapters of *Nudge*, Thaler and Sunstein introduce the historical context for their arguments by presenting two opposing schools of thought on human decision-making.

The first is the rational actor* model used in neoclassical economics. This has served as the bedrock of mainstream economic thinking since the post-World War II* era (the period from 1946). It proposes an abstract model of human behavior in which people behave completely rationally.

The second school of thought follows theories of behavioral economics. These ideas evolved in reaction to the rational actor model, which behavioral economists considered unrealistic. Behavioral economists aim to produce more realistic models of human decision-making based on psychological research into how people behave in the real world. This field was particularly influenced by work on flaws in human decision-making by Daniel Kahneman and Amos Tversky.

Nudge was published during the 2008 global financial crisis.* During that time, and in subsequent years, neoclassical economics was criticized by media figures[3] and academics[4] for its failure to foresee the crisis. In 2010, the Chicago–school economist Richard Posner* acknowledged that the crisis had created a "challenge to the economics profession as a whole, but to Chicago most of all."[5] The crisis led to an increased interest in behavioral economics as an alternative school of thought for understanding economic behavior.[6] In 2010, the future British prime minister, David Cameron, noted another consequence of the crisis, saying "the most important fact to bear in mind in British politics or American politics is: we have run out of money."[7] In that same talk, Cameron approvingly cited the ideas of behavioral economics as a way of achieving "a stronger society without necessarily having to spend a whole lot more money."[8] Both these factors helped create a more receptive atmosphere for the ideas of behavioral economics described in *Nudge*, particularly in the UK.

NOTES

1   Google Scholar records 5,495 texts which have cited *Nudge* as of September 26, 2015: https://scholar.google.com/scholar?cites=16854468477297806637&as_sdt=2005&sciodt=0,5&hl=en.

2   Richard H. Thaler and Cass R. Sunstein, *Nudge: Improving Decisions about Health, Wealth, and Happiness* (New York: Yale University Press, 2008), 5.

3   FT View, "Economics Needs to Reflect a Post-Crisis World," *Financial Times*, September 25, 2014, accessed October 15, 2015, http://www.ft.com/cms/s/0/f9f65e88-44a3-11e4-ab0c-00144feabdc0.html#axzz3ojq0z1zz.

4   Paul Krugman, "How Did Economists Get It So Wrong?," *New York Times*, September 6, 2009, accessed September 26, 2015, http://www.econ.ucdavis.edu/faculty/kdsalyer/LECTURES/Ecn200e/krugman_macro.pdf.

5   John Cassidy, "After the Blowup," *New Yorker*, January 11, 2010, accessed
     September 26, 2015, http://www.newyorker.com/magazine/2010/01/11/
     after-the-blowup.

6   "Behavioural Finance to the Rescue?" *Economist*, August 18, 2009,
     accessed September 26, 2015, http://www.economist.com/blogs/
     freeexchange/2009/08/behavioural_finance_to_the_res.

7   David Cameron, "The Next Age of Government," *TED*, February 2010,
     accessed September 4, 2015, http://www.ted.com/talks/david_
     cameron?language=en.

8   Cameron, "Next Age of Government."

MODULE 2
ACADEMIC CONTEXT

KEY POINTS

- The economic school of neoclassical economics* assumes a model of human decision-making in which people are perfectly rational.

- Thaler's insight, drawn from the work of the psychologists Kahneman* and Tversky,* was that sometimes people could consistently behave "irrationally" in a predictable way.

- Thaler integrated this insight into conventional economic thinking to become a founding figure in the field of behavioral economics.*

The Work in Its Context

Richard H. Thaler and Cass R. Sunstein's *Nudge: Improving Decisions about Health, Wealth, and Happiness* is grounded in the theories of behavioral economics. This discipline integrates research from psychology into economics with the goal of producing more realistic models of human decision-making. In their review of the history of behavioral economics, the American behavioral economists Colin Camerer* and George Loewenstein* identify Adam Smith's* 1759 book *The Theory of Moral Sentiments** as the foundational text of the discipline for its insights into the psychological principles of individual behavior.[1]

Camerer and Loewenstein date the modern discipline of behavioral economics as beginning in the second half of the twentieth century out of opposition to the use of rational choice theory* in neoclassical economics. That theory describes a simplified model of

❝ My greatest inspiration came from Kahneman and Tversky. ❞

Richard H. Thaler, quoted in Elina Halonen, "Research Heroes: Richard Thaler," *InDecision Blog*

human decision-making in which people behave as "rational actors,"* with complete information about the choices available to them, perfect cognitive ability, and infinite self-control. In *Nudge*, Thaler and Sunstein criticize these assumptions as unrealistic. They describe rational actors as people who "can think like Albert Einstein, store as much memory as IBM's [supercomputer] Big Blue, and exercise the willpower of [the Indian political leader] Mahatma Gandhi."[2]

Overview of the Field

While economists have long been aware of the criticisms of the rational choice theory,[3] one benefit was that it allowed them to make clear predictions about economic behavior. Many of these predictions were borne out by empirical evidence (evidence verifiable by observation) such as people buying less of a product when the price goes up, and working more when wages rise, suggesting that the model was broadly accurate in the long run when applied to large groups of people.

One economist who challenged the assumption of perfect rationality was the American Nobel Prize-winning economist Herbert Simon* who wrote several texts in the 1940s and 1950s suggesting that psychological factors constrained humans' ability to act in a fully rational way. Yet, in Thaler's words, "[Simon] had little impact on economics. And the reason is ... he didn't have systematic bias."[4] This is to say that Simon did not demonstrate that people would consistently act against the predictions of rational choice theory. Camerer and Loewenstein support Thaler's contention, saying that Simon's work "attracted attention, but did not alter the fundamental direction of economics."[5]

Academic Influences

Thaler's insight was that "there could be predictable bias."[6] By this he meant that sometimes people could consistently behave in a way that seemed "irrational" by the standards of rational choice theory.

He developed this idea from studying the work of Daniel Kahneman and Amos Tversky in the 1970s. During that decade, Kahneman and Tversky produced a series of seminal papers on human decision-making. Although Tversky died in in 1996, Kahneman won the Nobel Prize in Economics in 2002 for "having integrated insights from psychological research into economic science, especially concerning human judgment and decision-making under uncertainty."[7] One of their influential articles was "Judgment under Uncertainty: Heuristics and Biases," published in the journal *Science** in 1974. It argued that people often used mental shortcuts—called "heuristics"*—to make judgments: for example, the "availability heuristic"* whereby people often rely on examples that immediately spring to mind when making a judgment. A person using this heuristic might overestimate the risk of dying from a heart attack because they can readily recall a friend with heart problems, even if the statistical probability is objectively low.

Another influential paper by Kahneman and Tversky was "Prospect Theory,"* published in the economics journal *Econometrica** in 1979. Its insight was that people treated money differently depending on whether it was a gain or a loss. Consider a coin-toss—if heads, you win $20; if tails, you lose $20. Kahneman and Tversky found that most people would not take this bet. The participants in their experiments liked winning money, but strongly disliked losing it, a principle known as "loss aversion."*This contradicted the predictions of neoclassical assumptions, which assumed that people would treat gains and losses in the same way.

The availability heuristic and loss aversion, and many other heuristics and biases, showed that people could systematically behave "irrationally."

In the 1980s, Thaler began collecting other examples of behavioral biases in a column called "Anomalies"* in the respected *Journal of Economic Perspectives*.*[8] This column gave Thaler a small but influential platform to publicize the new field of behavioral economics to a mainstream economics audience. In Daniel Kahneman's view, "[Anomalies] got behavioral economics started as a field … it became respectable."[9]

NOTES

1   Colin F. Camerer and George Loewenstein, "Behavioral Economics: Past, Present, Future," in *Advances in Behavioral Economics*, ed. Colin F. Camerer et al. (Princeton, N.J.: Princeton University Press, 2003).

2   Richard H. Thaler and Cass R. Sunstein, *Nudge: Improving Decisions about Health, Wealth, and Happiness* (New York: Yale University Press, 2008), 6.

3   Gary Becker, "Irrational Behavior and Economic Theory," *Journal of Political Economy* 70, no. 1 (1962): 1–13.

4   Richard H. Thaler, "Do You Need a Nudge?" *Yale Insights*, November 4, 2009, accessed September 4, 2015, http://insights.som.yale.edu/insights/do-you-need-nudge.

5   Camerer and Loewenstein, "Behavioral Economics: Past, Present, Future," 5.

6   Thaler, "Do You Need a Nudge?"

7   "Sveriges Riksbank Prize in Economic Sciences in Memory of Alfred Nobel 2002," *Nobelprize.org*, accessed September 4, 2015, http://www.nobelprize.org/nobel_prizes/economic-sciences/laureates/2002/.

8   Richard H. Thaler's "Anomalies" columns are listed at http://faculty.chicagobooth.edu/Richard.Thaler/research/anomalies.html, accessed September 4, 2015.

9   Gregory Karp, "Profile: Richard Thaler, University of Chicago Booth School of Business Professor," *Chicago Tribune*, April 30, 2012, accessed September 4, 2015, http://articles.chicagotribune.com/2012-04-30/business/ct-biz-0430-executive-profile-thaler-20120430_1_economics-daniel-kahneman-cost-fallacy.

MODULE 3
THE PROBLEM

KEY POINTS

- *Nudge* was motivated by a belief that rational choice theory,* with its assumptions that economic decisions are made rationally, was inadequate for understanding many human behaviors.

- Research in behavioral economics* suggested that people often made "irrational" errors in decision-making.

- Thaler and Sunstein synthesized hundreds of studies in *Nudge* to argue that the theories of behavioral economics could offer a more realistic understanding of human behavior.

Core Question

Richard H. Thaler and Cass R. Sunstein's *Nudge: Improving Decisions about Health, Wealth and Human Happiness* was motivated by the authors' belief that the models of neoclassical economics,* in which people made rational choices based on complete information, were inadequate for understanding many human behaviors. Instead they proposed that the theories of behavioral economics could provide a more realistic understanding of human decision-making.

Richard Thaler was trained in neoclassical economic thinking during his PhD in the 1970s. He regarded rational choice theory as a good model of how people should behave, but not an accurate description of how they often did behave in the real world. In his words, "if you want a single, unified theory of economic behavior we already have the best one available, the selfish, rational agent model …

> ❝ In many cases, people make pretty bad decisions—
> decisions they would not have made if they had paid
> full attention and possessed complete information,
> unlimited cognitive abilities, and complete self-control. ❞
>
> Richard H. Thaler and Cass R. Sunstein, *Nudge: Improving Decisions about Health, Wealth, and Happiness*

the problem comes if, instead of trying to advise [people] how to make decisions, you are trying to predict what they will actually do."[1]

Thaler's skepticism is perhaps clarified by describing the full implications of perfect rationality. People do not make mistakes in a world of rational choice theory. They do not impulsively buy things they may later regret, [2] smoke when they want to quit,[3] fail to stick to diets,[4] choose a mortgage they cannot afford,[5] or open a business because of overconfidence.[6] They are immune to framing effects,[7] such as whether a hamburger is advertised as 90 percent fat or 10 percent fat-free. Social norms do not affect their judgment, like being told that 87 percent of people believe registering as an organ donor is the right thing to do.[8] Their minds are not susceptible to heuristics* and biases like loss aversion* (the tendency for people to more strongly prefer avoiding losses than receiving gains) or the availability heuristic* (a mental rule-of-thumb we use to evaluate how likely something is, based on how easily examples come to mind). Rational actors do not need help with their choices because they already make the best possible decision 100 percent of the time.

The Participants
By the time Thaler and Sunstein were writing *Nudge* in the 2000s, behavioral economics had documented a large body of psychological evidence showing that people did in fact often behave "irrationally" by the standards of rational choice theory.

In the field of finance, Richard Thaler and the economist Werner De Bondt* found that psychological biases influenced the functioning of the stock market.[9] In 1997, the American economist David Laibson* introduced an influential model arguing that limits on self-control could make people less likely to save for retirement.[10] In 2001, the economists Brigitte Madrian* and Dennis Shea* demonstrated that changing default rules could affect major economic behaviors. They found that automatically enrolling a group of US employees into a certain pension plan, while allowing them the choice to opt out, dramatically increased the rate of participation in the program.[11] In 2008, the same year *Nudge* was published, the business professor John Beshears* and colleagues documented ways in which the market would not necessarily make people behave rationally, as assumed in neoclassical economics.[12]

The Contemporary Debate

In *Nudge,* Thaler and Sunstein synthesized the results of hundreds of scientific articles published over several decades. Throughout the book, they emphasize the long history and cross-disciplinary nature of behavioral economics by discussing the work of their many contemporaries and predecessors who contributed to the discipline's understanding of human behavior.

While the evidence of these psychological studies has now been accepted into mainstream economics, economists differ in their views about the implications of this evidence. One recent undergraduate economics textbook says that "research in behavioral economics suggests that the neoclassical rationality axiom does not stand up to tests of logic, experience, or the needs of society."[13] Another textbook has a more skeptical reaction, arguing that "markets tend to reward rational behavior, while punishing irrationality. Even if many participants do not behave rationally, those who do behave sensibly will have the biggest effect on prices and outcomes."[14] In other words, individual examples of irrationality may not add up to important effects in the overall population.

Lastly, the behavioral economists Colin Camerer* and George Loewenstein* offer a balanced perspective, saying that "at the core of behavioral economics is the conviction that increasing the realism of the psychological underpinnings of economic analysis will improve economics on its own terms—generating theoretical insights, making better predictions of field phenomena, and suggesting better policy. This conviction does not imply a wholesale rejection of the neoclassical approach."[15]

NOTES

1   Richard H. Thaler, "When Will There Be a Single Unified 'Behavioral' Theory of Economic Activity?" in "What's the Question about Your Field That You Dread Being Asked?" *Edge*, March 28, 2013, accessed September 4, 2015, http://edge.org/conversation/whats-the-question-about-your-field-that-you-dread-being-asked#25056.

2   Richard H. Thaler and Cass R. Sunstein, *Nudge: Improving Decisions about Health, Wealth, and Happiness* (New York: Yale University Press, 2008), 51.

3   Thaler and Sunstein, *Nudge*, 44.

4   Thaler and Sunstein, *Nudge*, 7.

5   Thaler and Sunstein, *Nudge*, 134.

6   Thaler and Sunstein, *Nudge*, 32.

7   Thaler and Sunstein, *Nudge*, 36.

8   Thaler and Sunstein, *Nudge*, 182.

9   Werner F. M. De Bondt and Richard H. Thaler, "Does the Stock Market Overreact?" *Journal of Finance* 40, no. 3 (1985): 793–805.

10 David Laibson, "Golden Eggs and Hyperbolic Discounting," *Quarterly Journal of Economics* 112, no. 2 (1997): 443–78.

11 Brigitte C. Madrian and Dennis F. Shea, "The Power of Suggestion: Inertia in 401(k) Participation and Savings Behavior," *Quarterly Journal of Economics* 116, no. 4 (2001): 1149–87.

12 John Beshears et al., "How Are Preferences Revealed?" *Journal of Public Economics* 92 (2008): 1787–94.

13 Neva Goodwin et al., *Microeconomics in Context*, 3rd edn (Abingdon: Routledge, 2013), 155.

14 Hal Varian, *Intermediate Microeconomics*, 8th edn (New York: W. W. Norton & Company, 2009), 579.

15 Colin F. Camerer and George Loewenstein, "Behavioral Economics: Past, Present, Future," in *Advances in Behavioral Economics*, ed. Colin F. Camerer et al. (Princeton, NJ: Princeton University Press, 2003).

MODULE 4
THE AUTHORS' CONTRIBUTION

KEY POINTS

- Thaler and Sunstein's main argument in *Nudge* is that governments should help people to make better decisions without restricting their freedom of choice.

- Reconciling these contradictory goals was one of the main insights of *Nudge*.

- The author's philosophy of "libertarian paternalism"* — an idea founded on free choice (libertarianism*) and benevolent intervention (paternalism*) — built on work by themselves and their contemporaries in 2003.

Authors' Aims

Richard H. Thaler and Cass R. Sunstein use the opening chapters of *Nudge: Improving Decisions about Health, Wealth and Human Happiness* to establish that people's decision-making is often affected by psychological factors. They cite a large body of evidence showing that these factors can lead people to make poor decisions, supplementing this empirical evidence with anecdotes and personal observations about ways in which people think and behave irrationally.

After building their case, Thaler and Sunstein spell out its implications. They argue that governments should use the theories of behavioral economics* to help people make better decisions that would improve their lives. But they also stipulate that government intervention should not force people to make certain decisions, citing the words of the economist Milton Friedman* that people should be "free to choose."[1] They call this political philosophy "libertarian paternalism."

> ❝ We argue for self-conscious efforts, by institutions in the private sector and also by government, to steer people's choices in directions that will improve their lives. ❞
>
> Richard H. Thaler and Cass R. Sunstein, *Nudge: Improving Decisions about Health, Wealth, and Happiness*

Nudge's concept of limited government intervention to improve individual decision-making was not entirely novel—a similar argument was made in a 2003 article by the behavioral economist Colin Camerer* and colleagues.[2] However, one great success of the book was its presentation of the idea of "soft paternalism" to a lay audience in accessible language, while supporting the concept's rationale with an overwhelming body of scientific evidence.

Approach

Throughout *Nudge*, Thaler and Sunstein build their case for government intervention by citing the results of hundreds of scientific studies showing how psychological factors can negatively affect decision-making. Their combined expertise in behavioral economics and law made them well positioned to make this argument. Thaler was a founding figure in the field of behavioral economics and had systematically collected examples of deviations from rational behavior since the 1980s in his "Anomalies"* column in the *Journal of Economic Perspectives*.[3] Sunstein had written influential texts on how the principles of behavioral economics could apply to the law and explain people's interactions with the legal system. His expertise in governance and political philosophy helped provide *Nudge* with its coherent framework of government intervention.

Thaler and Sunstein first developed their ideas about government intervention in an article published in 2003 called "Libertarian

Paternalism is not an Oxymoron."[4] This title highlighted an apparent contradiction. Libertarianism is a political philosophy that emphasizes individual liberty and is hostile to government oversight. To be paternalistic means to act on a person's behalf for what you deem to be their own good, like a parent who forbids their child from eating fast food. Thaler and Sunstein reconciled this contradiction through a subtle argument. They proposed that interventions to help people make better choices were permissible, provided they respected individual freedom of choice. They give the example of a firm that wishes to encourage its workers to save more.[5] Rather than asking them to enroll in a pension plan, the firm assumes that they will wish to participate. It automatically enrolls all employees unless they specifically choose to opt out. The general tendency of people to stick with a default increases the savings rate, while those who wish to opt out are free to do so.

Contribution in Context

Although Thaler and Sunstein did not modify their idea of libertarian paternalism when it was included in *Nudge* five years later, they did present it in a different context. In their book, Thaler and Sunstein are much more explicit in selling the idea of libertarian paternalism to American readers by framing it in the context of US politics. They say that their approach could "serve as a viable middle ground in our unnecessarily polarized society"[6] and act as a "real third way"*[7] that could appeal to both Democrats* and Republicans* (that is, to people at different points on the political spectrum).

Thaler and Sunstein were not the only behavioral economists to make this argument. In 2003, the same year they introduced libertarian paternalism, the behavioral economist Colin Camerer and colleagues published a paper that introduced "asymmetric paternalism."[8] The two philosophies are essentially identical, reflecting the fact that they come from a common school of thought. However, Camerer and colleagues were more direct in framing the potential political application of their philosophy, as indicated by the article's title "Regulation for Conservatives."* That title implicitly acknowledges that since political liberals tend to be more open to government interventions, arguments for "nudge"*-like interventions may need to convince political conservatives in particular if they are to be broadly accepted.

NOTES

1   Richard H. Thaler and Cass R. Sunstein, *Nudge: Improving Decisions about Health, Wealth, and Happiness* (New York: Yale University Press, 2008), 5.

2   Colin Camerer et al., "Regulation for Conservatives: Behavioral Economics and the Case for 'Asymmetric Paternalism,'" *University of Pennsylvania Law Review* 151, no. 3 (2003): 1211–54.

3   Richard H. Thaler's "Anomalies" columns are listed at http://faculty. chicagobooth.edu/Richard.Thaler/research/anomalies.html, accessed September 4, 2015.

4   Richard H. Thaler and Cass R. Sunstein, "Libertarian Paternalism Is Not an Oxymoron," *University of Chicago Law Review* 70, no. 4 (2003): 1159–1202.

5   Thaler and Sunstein, *Nudge*, 109.

6   Thaler and Sunstein, *Nudge*, 252.

7   Thaler and Sunstein, *Nudge*, 252.

8   Camerer et al., "Regulation for Conservatives."

SECTION 2
IDEAS

MODULE 5
MAIN IDEAS

KEY POINTS

- There are two main themes in *Nudge*: how context can affect decision-making, and how governments can organize that context to help people make better choices without restricting freedom of choice.

- Thaler and Sunstein's main argument is that governments should "nudge"* people to make better decisions, as judged by the person themselves.

- The authors emphasize the applicability of their ideas to policy by providing specific examples of nudges in areas such as finance, health, and the environment.

Key Themes

Richard H. Thaler and Cass R. Sunstein's *Nudge: Improving Decisions about Health, Wealth and Human Happiness* is a book about human decision-making. In *Nudge*, Thaler and Sunstein examine two main themes on this topic:

- How context can affect decision-making
- How governments can organize that context to help people make better choices without restricting their freedom of choice.

Nudge's opening chapters describe the psychological factors that can sometimes affect decision-making; these include heuristics* (mental rules-of-thumb) and biases (tendencies toward certain interpretations of information), emotions and temptations, social pressures, and limits on cognitive ability (our ability to draw on our full intellectual capacity).

> **❝** A nudge ... alters people's behavior in a predictable way without forbidding any options or significantly changing their economic incentives. To count as a mere nudge, the intervention must be easy and cheap to avoid ... Putting fruit at eye level counts as a nudge. Banning junk food does not. **❞**
>
> Richard H. Thaler and Cass R. Sunstein, *Nudge: Improving Decisions about Health, Wealth, and Happiness*

Thaler and Sunstein argue that as a result of these factors, the context in which people make choices often causes them to make poor decisions. Thaler and Sunstein's proposed solution is for governments to organize the choice environment, without banning any options, so that people are more likely to act in their own self-judged best interest. They call this approach "nudging."

Exploring the Ideas

The authors' main contention is that the context in which people make decisions can affect their choices. They give the example of an online government program that required senior citizens to choose one of 47 different prescription-drug plans.[1] This complexity made it very difficult to choose the optimal plan. Designing the environment to influence behavior is what Thaler and Sunstein call "choice architecture."[*2] They argue that governments should create better choice architecture to help people make good decisions in many areas of life. However, they also believe that governments should not coerce people by denying them freedom of choice.

Changing the choice architecture to encourage a certain behavior, without banning any options, is what Thaler and Sunstein call a "nudge." In their words, "a nudge ... alters people's behavior in a predictable way without forbidding any options or significantly changing their economic incentives."[3] Everyday examples of nudges include: a satellite navigation system that helps drivers to their destination, a sign encouraging people to take the stairs instead of the elevator, a statement using a social norm to encourage a certain behavior ("most people pay their tax on time"), and government nutritional guidelines. In the context of an online drug prescription website, one effective nudge automatically assigned people a plan based on their historical prescription usage, while allowing them the option to choose a different plan.[4]

Throughout *Nudge*, Thaler and Sunstein ground their arguments by providing anecdotal examples and empirical evidence from scientific studies. They also provide many specific, practical examples of how governments and firms can use nudging to improve people's decision-making.

One example is the US "Save More Tomorrow" program that,[5] motivated by theoretical research in behavioral economics,* suggests procrastination prevents people from arranging their retirement plans. This program asked a firm's employees to specify the percentage of their future wages they wanted to contribute to their retirement fund. As a result, when they received pay rises, their contribution automatically rose. This overcame the problem of inertia (inaction) because employees no longer needed to actively manage and update their pension arrangements whenever they received a raise.

Another example concerns organ donation. Although surveys indicate that many people support organ donation, few sign up as organ donors. Thaler and Sunstein argue that the bureaucratic steps necessary to register deter people from signing up. They propose that "mandated choice" could address this gap between people's intentions and their behaviors.[6] This could be implemented on occasions when people are already interacting with the government, such as during a driving-license application. At that point drivers would be required to check a box stating their organ-donation preferences.

A final example is energy efficiency. A key challenge in this area is that most consumers are not able to judge how energy-efficient things are. The authors highlight the usefulness of information-disclosure laws in this context, such as a law that requires car companies to post in large print the fuel economy of their vehicles.[7] This is turn nudges consumers to purchase more efficient vehicles, if they so desire.

Language and Expression

Nudge is an accessible work that simultaneously targets general readers, academics, and policy-makers. Thaler and Sunstein communicate their main ideas using simple and amusing anecdotal examples, and build support for their arguments by citing quantitative evidence from scientific studies. They conclude with specific suggestions of how nudging can apply to many different areas of policy-making in the United States.

The authors introduced three new concepts in *Nudge*: "nudging," "choice architecture," and "libertarian paternalism."* The first two refer to the way the decision environment can be organized to encourage certain behaviors. The last describes the philosophy behind nudging, reconciling the contradictory idea of government acting on a person's behalf while respecting their freedom of choice. All three terms have become well known in academic and policy circles, showing the extent of the book's influence.

NOTES

1   Richard H. Thaler and Cass R. Sunstein, *Nudge: Improving Decisions about Health, Wealth, and Happiness* (New York: Yale University Press, 2008), 163.

2   Thaler and Sunstein, *Nudge*, 3.

3   Thaler and Sunstein, *Nudge*, 6.

4   Thaler and Sunstein, *Nudge*, 172.

5   Thaler and Sunstein, *Nudge*, 113.

6   Thaler and Sunstein, *Nudge*, 180.

7   Thaler and Sunstein, *Nudge*, 191.

MODULE 6
SECONDARY IDEAS

KEY POINTS

- There are two main secondary ideas in *Nudge*: that people use Automatic* (fast and instinctive) and Reflective (conscious and calculating) systems of thinking; and that people are already being constantly nudged* by the private sector.

- These ideas describe a mechanism for understanding how nudges work, and implicitly highlight a potential "dark side" of nudging.

- Thaler and Sunstein's argument that governments already nudge people through their existing choice architectures,* even if they do not intend to, may rebut a criticism the book later received.

Other Ideas

There are two main secondary ideas in Richard H. Thaler and Cass R. Sunstein's *Nudge: Improving Decisions about Health, Wealth and Human Happiness*:

- that people use Automatic and Reflective Systems of thinking
- that people experience nudges constantly in their day-to-day lives, whether the government intervenes or not.

The first idea is discussed early in *Nudge* as a way to frame the reader's understanding of how nudges work. Thaler and Sunstein discuss research from psychology and neuroscience that describes the functioning of the human brain. That approach conceives of two kinds of thinking: a fast and instinctive Automatic System, and a slower, more rational Reflective System.[1] Many of the nudges Thaler and Sunstein

> ❝ [Nudges] are the norm. We've been nudged forever. Eve and the serpent nudged Adam. Religions have been nudging us for thousands of years. Marketers nudge us. Ads are nudges. We can be nudged for good or for evil … We don't claim to have invented nudges. ❞
>
> Richard H. Thaler, "Do You Need a Nudge?" *Yale Insights*

cite throughout the book appear to work by targeting the Automatic System; in other words, by guiding people unconsciously rather than encouraging them to reflect more on their choices.

The second idea is that nudging is already pervasive in the real world in the form of advertising and sales techniques. Although Thaler and Sunstein only suggest nudges designed to improve human welfare, one subtext of the book is that it is easy to imagine "dark nudges" designed to encourage unhealthy habits or wasteful consumption.

Exploring the Ideas

Thaler and Sunstein use the concepts "Econs* and Humans" in *Nudge* to contrast how neoclassical* and behavioral economics*—one representing the mainstream orthodox approach to Western economic policy, the other an integration of research in the field of psychology and economic theory—describe human behavior. "Econs" are the perfectly rational beings described in rational choice theory.* "Humans" are real people, who occasionally make irrational decisions. Early in *Nudge*, Thaler and Sunstein relate these concepts to an influential psychological theory that describes people as having two systems of thinking. These are called the "Automatic" and "Reflective" Systems.[2] Also known as System 1 and System 2, these are discussed in greater detail by the Israeli psychologist Daniel Kahneman* in his book *Thinking, Fast and Slow.*[3]

The Automatic System is fast and instinctive. It is driven by feelings, habits, and triggers in the environment, and requires little to no cognitive engagement. It is how "Humans" often think. Some examples of Automatic thinking are:

- Knowing the answer to 2 + 2 without thinking
- Immediately recognizing a person is angry by their tone of voice and body language
- Effortlessly understanding short sentences in your native language.

The Reflective System is deliberative and rational. It is driven by values, knowledge, and intentions, and requires cognitive engagement. It is how "Econs" always think. Some examples of Reflective thinking are:

- Calculating the answer to 391 x 624
- Deciding what to study at university
- Understanding sentences in a foreign language by listening to them slowly and carefully.

Nudges often change behavior by targeting the Automatic System. They therefore affect Humans (who use this system) but not Econs (who do not). Examples include changing a default rule to an option that most people will prefer, framing choices in ways that make them more appealing, and simplifying complex choices to make them more understandable. All these nudges reduce cognitive burden and, as Thaler and Sunstein put it, "make it easier for people to go their own way."[4]

Another secondary idea in *Nudge* is the pervasiveness of nudges in our daily lives. A subtext of this is that these "nudges" may not have one's best interests at heart. For example, one book review has called nudging "a marketer's dream."[5] Firms in sales and advertising have used some of the techniques described in *Nudge* for decades, in the form of product placements and celebrity endorsements. The American technology firm Apple's iBeacon product is an example of nudge techniques applied to modern advertising. The journalist Nina Zipkin describes how iBeacon can track the movements of customers in US stores via their smartphone, down to the location of the aisle they are standing in.[6] This information can be used to personalize a shopping experience by providing micro-level notifications about deals on products in the customer's eye-line.

Overlooked

One subtle argument Thaler and Sunstein make in *Nudge* is that governments are already nudging their citizens, even if they don't intend to. In their words, "choice architecture and its effects cannot be avoided."[7]

After the book's publication, this argument was overlooked by critics who argued that *Nudge* was too paternalistic—that is, it proposed an excessive level of benevolent intervention in the life of the citizen. Sunstein's response was that "whenever a government has websites, communicates with its citizens, operates cafeterias, or maintains offices that people will visit, it nudges, whether or not it intends to."[8] His point was that existing choice architectures do not have a "neutral" default setting. One way or another, governments are already influencing their citizens' behavior through the structure of their existing institutions.

An implication of Sunstein's argument is that governments should therefore structure those institutions so that people are nudged toward better outcomes (as judged by themselves). Sunstein later expanded on this point in his book *Simpler*,[9] which discussed his three-year tenure as administrator of the Office of Information and Regulatory Affairs. In that book he emphasizes the importance of simplifying existing government forms and structures to improve their efficacy.

NOTES

1   Richard H. Thaler and Cass R. Sunstein, *Nudge: Improving Decisions about Health, Wealth, and Happiness* (New York: Yale University Press, 2008), 19.

2   Thaler and Sunstein, *Nudge*, 19.

3   Daniel Kahneman, *Thinking, Fast and Slow* (New York: Farrar, Straus and Giroux, 2011).

4   Thaler and Sunstein, *Nudge*, 5.

5   Jeremy Waldron, "It's All for Your Own Good," *New York Review of Books*, October 9, 2014, accessed September 4, 2015, http://www.nybooks.com/articles/archives/2014/oct/09/cass-sunstein-its-all-your-own-good/.

6   Nina Zipkin, "Attention, Apple Shoppers: You're Being Followed," December 6, 2013, accessed September 4, 2015, http://www.entrepreneur.com/article/230275.

7   Thaler and Sunstein, *Nudge*, 72.

8   Cass R. Sunstein, "There's a Backlash against Nudging—But It Was Never Meant to Solve Every Problem," *Guardian*, April 24, 2014, accessed September 4, 2015, http://www.theguardian.com/commentisfree/2014/apr/24/nudge-backlash-free-society-dignity-coercion.

9   Cass R. Sunstein, *Simpler: The Future of Government* (New York: Simon & Schuster, 2013).

MODULE 7
ACHIEVEMENT

KEY POINTS

- *Nudge* was well received by the public, academics, and policymakers.

- The book's success was helped by its impressive body of scientific evidence, its many practical examples of nudges,* and the timing of its publication.

- While nudges can improve decision-making, their main limitation is that they cannot address major societal challenges.

Assessing the Argument

In *Nudge: Improving Decisions about Health, Wealth, and Happiness*, Richard H. Thaler and Cass R. Sunstein make a convincing case that governments should "nudge" their citizens to make better decisions. The book's summary of decades of research from behavioral economics* and psychology, combined with its accessible writing style, helped make it a major success among the public, academics, and policy-makers.

The book's seemingly more realistic view of human decision-making contrasted with the more abstract, theoretical assumptions of neoclassical economics.* *Nudge's* positive reception was likely encouraged by the fact that it was published in mid-2008, a time when many people regarded neoclassical economic thinking as discredited by its failure to predict that year's financial crisis, as noted in one book review.[1]

Within academia, the book's concepts of "choice architecture"* and "nudging" were quickly adopted by other disciplines interested in behavior change. For example, public-health researchers have examined whether nudging can improve the health of large

> **❝Thaler and Sunstein have written an important book. ❞**
>
> Thomas C. Leonard, "Richard H. Thaler, Cass R. Sunstein, 'Nudge: Improving Decisions about Health, Wealth, and Happiness,'" *Constitutional Political Economy Book Review*

populations by reducing smoking, obesity, and physical inactivity.[2] Marketers have applied the book's ideas to influencing consumer behavior,[3] and political scientists have examined whether nudging can encourage civic behavior, such as voting.[4]

Achievement in Context

Nudge's ideas of light-touch government regulation and seemingly common-sense policy solutions appealed to many readers.[5] As well as being a popular best seller, Thaler and Sunstein's book affected real-world policy-making. Nudges were seen as particularly attractive policy options in the United Kingdom, partly because they were relatively cheap to implement at a time when the government was cutting spending in response to the 2008 financial crisis.*[6] The ideas contained in *Nudge* were quickly embraced by the right-wing Conservative party.* Three months after the book's publication, Conservative MP and future chancellor of the exchequer (financial minister) George Osborne* praised *Nudge* in the *Guardian* newspaper.[7] In 2010 the Conservative leader David Cameron,* by then prime minister, created the world's first Nudge Unit* to help government officials implement the book's ideas. In the five years since its creation, the Nudge Unit has published several papers documenting its interventions in many different policy areas, including taxation, unemployment, and charitable giving, further emphasizing the book's impact.[8]

In the United States, the success of *Nudge* inspired the creation of the Social and Behavioral Sciences Team.* This group was formally created by an executive order of President Barack Obama* in September 2015 which stated that "research findings from fields such as behavioral economics and psychology about how people make decisions and act on them ... can be used to design government policies to better serve the American people."[9] That executive order was accompanied by a report describing the team's recent interventions. Some of their successful nudges include using personalized text messages to improve college enrollment rates among low-income students; simplifying governmental debt-collection letters to increase the number of people paying online; and improving the accuracy of self-reported sales figures by vendors selling goods to the government by requiring their signature at the top of an online form (thereby prompting more honest responses).[10]

Limitations

A key strength of *Nudge* is the universality of its concepts of "choice architecture" and "nudging." Because these relate to how people fundamentally make decisions, the book's ideas can easily apply to different countries and contexts.

Despite this strength, the concept of nudging is limited in one crucial way. Nudges must be "easy and cheap to avoid."[11] They do not allow more conventional policy tools like taxation and regulation. This limitation was highlighted in 2009 by the British politician Ed Miliband,* the future leader of the center–left Labour party,* who criticized the idea of nudge policies at a time when Britain was in recession. He argued that "*Nudge* was very fashionable ... for a few months before the financial crisis. *Nudge* was about not really needing the state to do big things ... People don't talk about *Nudge* much any more."[12]

While Miliband was arguably incorrect in his assessment that *Nudge* was just a passing fad, given the book's continued influence on policy-making in the UK and US in the years since he made his remarks, he was probably correct that nudges cannot match traditional policy tools for addressing major challenges like economic recessions. A useful contrast to the relatively incremental adjustments in policy suggested by *Nudge* is the $831 billion in economic stimulus the US government spent in response to the 2008 financial crisis. This intervention would have been forbidden under the principles of *Nudge*, as would other large-scale government responses to challenges like obesity and climate change.

NOTES

1   Joel Anderson, "Review of *Nudge: Improving Decisions and Health, Wealth, and Happiness*," *Economics and Philosophy* 26, no. 3 (2010): 369–76.

2   Theresa M. Marteau et al., "Judging Nudging: Can Nudging Improve Population Health?" *British Medical Journal* 342 (2011).

3   Daniel G. Goldstein et al., "Nudge Your Customers toward Better Choices," *Harvard Business Review*, December 2008, accessed September 4, 2015, https://hbr.org/2008/12/nudge-your-customers-toward-better-choices.

4   David W. Nickerson and Todd Rogers, "Do You Have a Voting Plan? Implementation Intentions, Voter Turnout, and Organic Plan Making," *Psychological Science* 21, no. 2 (2010): 194–9.

5   Benjamin M. Friedman, "Guiding Forces," *New York Times*, August 22, 2008, accessed September 5, 2015, http://www.nytimes.com/2008/08/24/books/review/Friedman-t.html?pagewanted=all&_r=0.

6   David Cameron, "The Next Age of Government," *TED*, February 2010, accessed September 4, 2015, http://www.ted.com/talks/david_cameron?language=en.

7   George Osborne, "Nudge, Nudge, Win, Win," *Guardian*, July 14, 2008, accessed September 4, 2015, http://www.theguardian.com/commentisfree/2008/jul/14/conservatives.economy.

8   Behavioural Insights Team, "The Behavioural Insights Team Update report 2013–2015," accessed September 4, 2015, http://www.behaviouralinsights.co.uk/wp-content/uploads/2015/07/BIT_Update-Report-Final-2013–2015.pdf.

9   The White House, "Executive Order—Using Behavioral Science Insights to Better Serve the American People," *Office of the Press Secretary*, September 15, 2015, accessed September 30, 2015, https://www.whitehouse.gov/the-press-office/2015/09/15/executive-order-using-behavioral-science-insights-better-serve-american.

10 Social and Behavioral Sciences Team, "Social and Behavioral Sciences Team Annual Report," *Executive Office of the President National Science and Technology Council*, September 2015, accessed September 30, 2015, https://www.whitehouse.gov/sites/default/files/microsites/ostp/sbst_2015_annual_report_final_9_14_15.pdf.

11 Richard H. Thaler and Cass R. Sunstein, *Nudge: Improving Decisions about Health, Wealth, and Happiness* (New York: Yale University Press, 2008), 6.

12 Andrew Sparrow, "Fabian Conference—Live," *Guardian*, January 17, 2009, accessed September 4, 2015, http://www.theguardian.com/politics/blog/2009/jan/17/fabian-conference-blog.

MODULE 8
PLACE IN THE AUTHORS' WORK

KEY POINTS

- Throughout their careers, Thaler and Sunstein have applied ideas from psychology and behavioral economics* to understanding human decision-making.

- Although Thaler and Sunstein were distinguished scholars before *Nudge*, the book hugely increased their profile and remains their biggest success.

- The book's accomplishment represented a culmination of Thaler's life's work by introducing the field of behavioral economics to a global audience.

Positioning

When *Nudge: Improving Decisions about Health, Wealth, and Happiness* was published in 2008, Richard H. Thaler and Cass R. Sunstein had each worked in academia for three decades. Both held professorships at the University of Chicago and had produced important and widely cited work, applying the principles of behavioral economics to finance and law. In spite of these achievements, *Nudge* was the biggest success of both authors' careers. It became an internationally acclaimed best seller, directly influenced government policy-making in some of the world's most advanced countries, and continues to be highly cited by many academic disciplines.

The ideas in *Nudge* reflected the authors' long-standing interest in applying theories from behavioral economics and psychology to improve human decision-making. In 1998, they collaborated with the American law professor Christine Jolls* to describe how behavioral economics could provide more realistic theories of law and

> ❝ Libertarian paternalism provides a basis for both understanding and rethinking a number of areas of contemporary law, including those aspects that deal with worker welfare, consumer protection, and the family. ❞
>
> Richard H. Thaler and Cass R. Sunstein, "Libertarian Paternalism Is Not an Oxymoron," *University of Chicago Law Review*

government.[1] In 2003, they described how libertarian paternalism* could inform government policy-making in an article published in *The University of Chicago Law Review*.[2] That article, "Libertarian Paternalism Is Not an Oxymoron," concluded that their philosophy provided "a foundation for rethinking many areas of private and public law."[3]

Thaler and Sunstein later expanded their argument from that 44-page article into the 293 pages of *Nudge*. Their book-length treatment fleshed out their argument in several ways, giving a more complete description of the many psychological studies that informed their ideas about decision-making. They provided more examples of "nudges"* and described how the concept could be used in the context of American politics. The accessible language in the book also made it appealing to a non-academic audience.

Integration

Thaler's overall body of work can be considered coherent. He has consistently written on behavioral economics throughout his career. Sunstein's writing is less unified because his academic interests are wide-ranging. He has published most frequently on law and governance but also on more esoteric topics such as animal rights, conspiracy theories, and political extremism. He is famously prolific—as of 2015 he is credited with almost 500 publications, including books, academic articles, and media pieces.

Bringing behavioral economics to global prominence, *Nudge* represents the culmination of Thaler's life's work. He is the author of many the most important papers in the field and, in the 1980s and 1990s, introduced its ideas to a mainstream economics audience through his column "Anomalies"* in the *Journal of Economic Perspectives.** In consequence, the Nobel Prize-winning psychologist Daniel Kahneman* has called Thaler the "person who really created behavioral economics."[4] *Nudge's* best-selling, influential status confirmed the growth of behavioral economics from a discipline initially treated with contempt by many economists[5] to a respected field that offers important insights into human behavior.

Nudge is also an effective summary of Sunstein's body of work, examining how behavioral economics can inform theories of law and governance. The concept of nudging—which typically emphasizes incremental, case-specific modifications of existing policies—is consistent with Sunstein's writings on "judicial minimalism,"* a legal philosophy that favors case-by-case adjudication rather than major overhauls on matters of constitutional law.*

Significance

Many academics today consider Thaler a likely future winner of the Nobel Prize in Economics, based on work he had done before *Nudge* was published.[6] Sunstein is one of the most cited legal scholars in the world and was one of the highest officials of the Obama administration* during his three-year tenure as administrator of the Office of Information and Regulatory Affairs. Despite these existing accomplishments, the success of *Nudge* elevated both authors to a new global prominence.

Nudge's most dramatic real-world impact has been its effect on policy-making around the world. *Nudge's* philosophy of light-touch regulation strongly appealed to the Conservative party* in the United Kingdom. In 2010, a mere two years after *Nudge* was published, David

Cameron, prime minister of a Conservative-led administration, put the book's ideas into practice by creating the world's first governmental Nudge Unit.* The success of that group has since inspired the creation of the Social and Behavioral Sciences Team* in the United States and influenced policy-makers in Germany, the Netherlands, Finland, Singapore, and Australia.[7]

The ideas in *Nudge* also inspired the creation of the "world's first public policy behavioural insights conference" in 2014.[8] The success of the Behavioural Exchange conference, now an annual event, is a clear sign of the continuing interest in *Nudge* from academics, policy-makers, and the media.

NOTES

1   Christine Jolls et al., "A Behavioral Approach to Law and Economics," *Stanford Law Review* 50, no. 5 (1998): 1471–550.

2   Richard H. Thaler and Cass R. Sunstein, "Libertarian Paternalism Is Not an Oxymoron," *University of Chicago Law Review* 70, no. 4 (2003).

3   Sunstein and Thaler, "Libertarian Paternalism," 1202.

4   Morgan Housel, "Daniel Kahneman on Challenging Economic Assumptions," *Motley Fool*, June 29, 2013, accessed September 4, 2015, http://www.fool.com/investing/general/2013/06/29/challenging-assumptions-an-economist-considers-psy.aspx.

5   Housel, "Daniel Kahneman."

6   Noah Smith, "Five Economists Who Deserve Nobels," *Bloomberg View*, December 9, 2014, accessed September 4, 2015, http://www.bloombergview.com/articles/2014-12–09/five-economists-who-deserve-nobels.

7   Behavioural Insights Team, "The Behavioural Insights Team Update Report 2013–2015," accessed September 4, 2015, http://www.behaviouralinsights.co.uk/wp-content/uploads/2015/07/BIT_Update-Report-Final-2013–2015.pdf.

8   Behavioural Insights Team, "Behavioural Exchange 2014," accessed September 30, 2015, http://www.behaviouralinsights.co.uk/bx2015/behavioural-exchange-2014/.

SECTION 3
IMPACT

MODULE 9
THE FIRST RESPONSES

KEY POINTS

- *Nudge* received two main criticisms: that nudges* were too paternalistic; that nudges could only change behavior in a superficial way.

- Thaler and Sunstein responded to their critics through interviews and articles.

- Thaler and Sunstein conceded that nudging alone could not fix major societal problems, but they did not change their essential positions.

Criticism

Richard H. Thaler and Cass R. Sunstein's *Nudge: Improving Decisions about Health, Wealth and Human Happiness* became an international best seller and was named one of the best books of 2008 by the British periodical the *Economist*[1] and by the *Financial Times*[2] newspaper. Despite its success, *Nudge* also received criticism from media figures and academics.

The first criticism was that nudging was too paternalistic, as exemplified in an argument between Thaler and the American economist Richard Posner* shortly after *Nudge* was published. The point of contention was the US Consumer Financial Protection Agency,* a body set up in response to the 2008 financial crisis.* Influenced by research in behavioral economics, one of its goals was to protect consumers from financial abuse by using "actual data about how people make financial decisions."[3] It required financial institutions to offer customers simple "vanilla" (that is, unchallenging and "everyday") mortgages whose conditions could be read in less

> **❝** Our central finding is that non-regulatory measures
> used in isolation, including 'nudges,' are less likely to
> be effective. Effective policies often use a range of
> interventions. **❞**
>
> House of Lords Science and Technology Select Committee, "Behaviour
> Change Report"

than three minutes. Posner harshly criticized this proposal in the *Wall Street Journal*.[4] He argued that vanilla products would make sellers fearful of offering other types of mortgages. This would reduce competition in the market and make customers worse off.

The second critique was that nudges were too superficial to address major societal challenges. This criticism was detailed in a report on behavior change by the House of Lords (the higher of the British Parliament's two governmental law-making bodies). Baroness Julia Neuberger,* heading that report, argued that serious behavior change required "more than just nudge … behavioural change interventions appear to work best when they're part of a package of regulation and fiscal measures."[5] The report cited obesity as a societal challenge influenced by complex social and environmental factors that should therefore be addressed by a combination of policy measures rather than just individual-level nudges.[6]

Responses

Since *Nudge*'s publication, Thaler and Sunstein have responded to their critics through a large number of interviews and articles.

Thaler rejected Posner's argument over mortgages as misleading, in an article published in *PBS Newshour*.[7] He argued that vanilla financial products would not restrict consumer choice but would provide a baseline against which customers could judge other products. Firms would be free to offer more complicated products for people who wanted them. Thaler compared the idea of a vanilla mortgage to the standard lease used in rental agreements that provides a framework for consumers to identify whether a landlord is offering them unusual terms. This frame of reference helps them to judge whether the nonstandard terms are in their best interest.

In a *Guardian* article, Sunstein acknowledged that nudging alone could not fix society's biggest challenges, saying, "nudges are not a sufficient approach to some of our most serious problems, such as violent crime, poverty, and climate change … No one denies that requirements and bans have their place."[8] Thaler and Sunstein have never themselves claimed nudging could solve these kinds of problems. This criticism may be more fairly directed at policy-makers who neglect conventional policy tools, like taxation and regulation, in favor of nudging because the former are more difficult to implement.

Conflict and Consensus

Thaler and Sunstein countered many initial criticisms of *Nudge* by carefully reiterating the book's core arguments. They repeated that true nudges did not restrict freedom of choice and that policymakers who did so were not adhering to libertarian paternalism. They admitted that nudges alone could not solve all of society's problems—but they themselves had never made this claim.

Subsequent debates advanced subtler arguments that were not as easily refuted. One criticism was that nudges often exploit the same flaws in decision-making that they were designed to ameliorate. In other words, nudges often work by targeting the fast and instinctive Automatic System* instead of the slow and deliberative Reflective System. This point was raised in a review of *Nudge* in the *New York Review of Books*.[9] The reviewer concluded that he would prefer nudges that made him a consciously better chooser rather than an unconsciously guided one. Although Sunstein responded to the author's other criticisms, he did not address this point.[10]

NOTES

1 "Pick of the Pile," *Economist*, December 4, 2008, accessed September 4, 2015, http://www.economist.com/node/12719711.

2 "Best Business Books," *Financial Times*, 2008, accessed September 4, 2015, http://ig.ft.com/sites/business-book-award/books/2008/longlist/nudge-by-richard-thaler-and-cass-sunstein.

3 "Executive Summary of Financial Regulatory Reform: A New Foundation," *US Treasury Department*, June 17, 2009, accessed September 4, 2015, http://www.treasury.gov/initiatives/wsr/Documents/executive_summary.pdf.

4 Richard A. Posner, "Treating Financial Consumers as Consenting Adults," *Wall Street Journal*, July 22, 2009, accessed September 4, 2015, http://www.wsj.com/articles/SB10001424052970203946904574302213213148166.

5 Elizabeth Day, "Julia Neuberger: 'A Nudge in the Right Direction Won't Run the Big Society,'" *Observer*, July 17, 2011, accessed September 4, 2015, http://www.theguardian.com/society/2011/jul/17/julia-neuberger-nudge-big-society.

6 House of Lords Science and Technology Select Committee, "Behaviour Change Report," *HL Paper* 179, (2011): 52–7, accessed September 4, 2015, http://www.publications.parliament.uk/pa/ld201012/ldselect/ldsctech/179/179.pdf.

7 Richard Thaler, "Thaler Responds to Posner on Consumer Protection," *PBS Newshour*, July 28, 2009, accessed September 4, 2015, http://www.pbs.org/newshour/making-sense/thaler-responds-to-posner-on-c/.

8 Cass R. Sunstein, "There's a Backlash against Nudging—But It Was Never Meant to Solve Every Problem," *Guardian*, April 24, 2014, accessed September 4, 2015, http://www.theguardian.com/commentisfree/2014/apr/24/nudge-backlash-free-society-dignity-coercion.

9 Jeremy Waldron, "It's All for Your Own Good," New York Review of Books, October 9, 2014, http://www.nybooks.com/articles/archives/2014/oct/09/cass-sunstein-its-all-your-own-good/, accessed September 4, 2015.

10 Cass R. Sunstein, "Nudges: Good and Bad," New York Review of Books, October 23, 2014, accessed September 4, 2015, http://www.nybooks.com/articles/archives/2014/oct/23/nudges-good-and-bad/.

MODULE 10
THE EVOLVING DEBATE

KEY POINTS

- The term "nudging"* is now commonly used by academics and global policymakers.

- Sunstein's book *Why Nudge?* summarizes the authors' responses to the criticisms the book has accumulated.

- The success of *Nudge* has led to many interventions being incorrectly described as "behavioral economics."* There is now a move toward broader terms such as "behavioral science"* and "behavioral insights."

Uses and Problems

Richard H. Thaler and Cass R. Sunstein's argument in *Nudge: Improving Decisions about Health, Wealth, and Happiness* that governments should nudge their citizens has been broadly accepted by many policymakers and academics. There are two noticeable trends in the current debate.

The first is the continued critiques of the book's ideas. One criticism by the Belgian philosopher Luc Bovens* is that nudges are dangerous because they are subtle.[1] People do not notice them in the way they notice bans or regulation, so bad nudges might not trigger the same political response as bad regulations. Another criticism is that *Nudge* identifies consistent flaws in human decision-making—but policymakers are, of course, subject to the same flaws. How, then, can the public trust them to make sensible interventions?[2] A further criticism is that because nudges are designed to discourage people from making bad choices, they make it less likely that people will learn from their mistakes.

> **66** The whole point of a nudge, and of creating the Behavioural Insights Teams in the UK and now others around the world, was to give non-economists a voice in designing policy. **99**
>
> Richard Thaler quoted in Peter Ubel, "Q & A with Richard Thaler on What It Really Means to Be a 'Nudge,'" *Forbes*

Sunstein's book *Why Nudge?*[3] contains his responses to the long list of criticisms *Nudge* has received. The American psychologist Barry Schwartz* concluded in his review of *Why Nudge?* that it was "nuanced and sophisticated in its arguments."[4]

The second trend is an unexpected consequence of *Nudge*'s enormous success—behavior change has become too closely identified with behavioral economics in the popular media. Daniel Kahneman* discusses this in *The Behavioral Foundations of Public Policy*.[5] For him, many applications of cognitive and social psychology to policy have been incorrectly called "behavioral economics." Thaler himself, he adds, "has always insisted on a narrow definition of behavioral economics and … would prefer to see 'nudges' described as applications of behavioral science."[6]

This may seem just a superficial debate about labeling. Its broader implication is that the success of *Nudge* has legitimized the ability of psychology, and other disciplines in the social sciences, to contribute to policy-making. However, this represents a major shift, given that economics has traditionally been the only academic field that seriously affects policy-making. There are now conscious efforts to use broader terms such as "behavioral science" to describe behavioral change interventions.

Schools of Thought
Nudge has achieved the status of a distinct school of thought. The term "nudging" has entered the language of academics and policy-

makers, and some of the most influential organizations in the world now apply the book's ideas. For example, the report *Mind, Society and Behavior* from the Washington-based global financial institution the World Bank* discusses how nudging can be used in the developing world in areas like microfinance (a type of financial service targeted at individuals and small groups who lack access to traditional banking services) and testing for HIV (the virus that causes the immune system disease AIDS).[7] In 2013 the Financial Conduct Authority,* the UK's financial regulator, published a report describing how behavioral economics and nudging inform its work.[8] The behavioral economist Pete Lunn* has written for the Organization for Economic Co-operation and Development (OECD*)—a group of countries that promote democracy and economic growth by means of the market economy system—on the topic of behavioral economics and regulatory policy (policy formulated for purposes such as responding to financial crises or planning public investment).[9]

The 5,000 citations *Nudge* has received is a clear sign of its influence in the academic world.[10] Even more impressively, these citations have come from a diverse set of disciplines, including economics, psychology, public health, marketing, sociology, medicine, political science, criminology, and philosophy.

In Current Scholarship

The most influential group disseminating the ideas of *Nudge* today is arguably the Behavioural Insights Team* in the United Kingdom. This group—also called the Nudge Unit—was set up by Prime Minister David Cameron* in 2010 to implement the book's ideas in the new Conservative-led government. Richard Thaler is an external advisor to the team, demonstrating his continued influence.

The group's stated objectives are clearly inspired by *Nudge*. These are to "[enable] people to make 'better choices for themselves'," to "make public services more cost-effective and easier for citizens to use," and to "[introduce] a more realistic model of human behaviour to policy."[11] However, there are also signs that while the group has adopted the ideas of *Nudge*, it is not defined by them. On their website, the team do not use the word "nudge" to describe their approach, and their formal name uses the more general term "behavioural insights" instead of "behavioral economics." This mirrors the trend discussed by Kahneman of moving toward a broader approach to behavioral interventions that is not tied to the ideas of behavioral economics.

NOTES

1 Luc Bovens, "The Ethics of Nudge," in *Preference Change: Approaches from Philosophy, Economics and Psychology*, ed. Till Grüne-Yanoff and Sven Ove Hansson (New York: Springer, 2009), 207–19.

2 Jan Schnellenbach and Christian Schubert, "Behavioral Political Economy: A Survey," *European Journal of Political Economy*, in press (2015).

3 Cass R. Sunstein, *Why Nudge?* (New York: Yale University Press, 2014).

4 Barry Schwartz, "Why Not Nudge? A Review of Cass Sunstein's *Why Nudge?*" *thepsychreport,* April 17, 2014, accessed September 4, 2015, http://thepsychreport.com/essays-discussion/nudge-review-cass-sunsteins-why-nudge/.

5 Eldar Shafir, ed., *The Behavioral Foundations of Public Policy* (Princeton, N.J.: Princeton University Press, 2012), 7.

6 Shafir, *Behavioural Foundations*, 7.

7 World Bank, "Mind, Society, and Behavior," *World Bank Group Flagship Report*, 2015, accessed September 26, 2015, http://www.worldbank.org/content/dam/Worldbank/Publications/WDR/WDR%202015/WDR-2015-Full-Report.pdf.

8 Kristine Erta et al., "Applying Behavioural Economics at the Financial Conduct Authority," *FCA Occasional Paper* no. 1 (2013), accessed September 4, 2015, https://www.fca.org.uk/static/documents/occasional-papers/occasional-paper-1.pdf.

9 Pete Lunn, *Regulatory Policy and Behavioural Economics* (Paris: OECD Publishing, 2014).

10 Google Scholar records 5,495 texts which have cited *Nudge* as of September 26, 2015: https://scholar.google.com/scholar?cites= 16854468477297806637&as_sdt=2005&sciodt=0,5&hl=en.

11 Behavioural Insights Team, "Who We Are," accessed September 4, 2015, http://www.behaviouralinsights.co.uk/about-us/.

MODULE 11
IMPACT AND INFLUENCE TODAY

KEY POINTS

- *Nudge* has become a key reference for anyone interested in decision-making and public policy.

- By highlighting the contributions of behavioral economics* and psychology to understanding human behavior, the book challenges the dominance of neoclassical economics* as the only discipline capable of influencing policy.

- While *Nudge* has received criticism, its ideas have mostly been accepted by policymakers, business people, and academics.

Position

Less than 10 years after the publication of Richard H. Thaler and Cass R. Sunstein's *Nudge: Improving Decisions about Health, Wealth, and Happiness*, the book has become a key reference text for people in policy, academia, and business who are interested in decision-making and behavior change. Although *Nudge* has received considerable criticism, this is partly because the book's success and global influence have made it a very visible target. Sunstein's comprehensive response to these criticisms in *Why Nudge?* suggests that the ideas of choice architecture* and nudging* will continue to be influential for years to come.

Nudge has challenged the traditional dominance of neoclassical economics in policy-making. Despite their prominence in the field of behavioral economics, both Thaler and Sunstein have argued that psychological research in general should play a greater role in policy debates. Sunstein makes this point by highlighting that the US

> **❝** Politicians will only succeed if they ... treat people as they are, rather than as they would like them to be. If you combine this very simple, very conservative thought—go with the grain of human nature—with all the advances in behavioral economics ... I think we can achieve a real increase in well-being, in happiness, in a stronger society. **❞**
>
> David Cameron, "Next Age of Government," *TED*

president has a Council of Economic Advisers, but not a Council of Psychological Advisers.[1] To this end both have argued for the use of the broader term "behavioral science."*

Interaction

The success of *Nudge* and its promotion of behavioral science has dramatically affected policy-making in the United Kingdom. Between 2010 and 2015 the Behavioural Insights Team* (the Nudge Unit) published over a dozen papers documenting its *Nudge*-inspired interventions in policy areas such as the labor market, energy use, fraud, taxation, organ donation, and charitable giving. Some of its successes include:

- Generating millions of pounds in additional tax revenue by rewriting tax letters to include phrases like "Nine out of ten people in your town pay their taxes on time."[2] This intervention drew on research from psychology about how social norms affect behavior.
- Designing a successful program to help unemployed individuals return to employment. This program asked job-seekers to specify how they would search for a job instead of reporting on what activities they had undertaken. It also included an expressive writing component that asked individuals to identify their personal strengths.[3]

- Increasing the number of organ donors in the UK by nudging people to sign up after they renewed their driving licenses online.[4]

The success of the Behavioral Insights Team has provided a major publicity boost to the concept of policy-making that is informed by behavioral science and scientific methodology. The group's director, David Halpern,* has indicated that he sees their approach as the way of the future, saying, "I think we'll look back on this in a decade or two and say, 'You mean we didn't use to do this?'"[5]

The Continuing Debate

Nudge has produced diverse responses in the academic world. The British health psychologist Susan Michie* has been a noted critic of the limitations of nudging for changing health behaviors. She highlights that behaviors such as smoking and obesity are usually influenced by community- and population-level factors, rather than just the individual factors that nudging typically targets. For example, nudging an obese person to drink less soda may be ineffective for weight loss if the person lives in an environment that encourages unhealthy eating. Michie has introduced the Behaviour Change Wheel that provides a more detailed framework for designing interventions by taking into account these multi-level factors.[6]

How has mainstream economics reacted to *Nudge*? The book is rooted in the field of behavioral economics, which evolved as a response to the unrealistic assumptions about human behavior made in neoclassical economics. Kahneman* has said "the assumptions have been challenged, but economics is still pretty much the same discipline it was."[7] This may be too pessimistic. The behavioral economists Colin Camerer* and George Loewenstein* argue that behavioral economics is not a revolution that will replace neoclassical economics; instead, its ideas will be absorbed into neoclassical economic thinking.[8] Perhaps the most valuable change it has made is to suggest that the "one size fits all" rational actor* model, according to which we make economic decisions rationally in the light of the information we possess, is not always an appropriate tool for understanding human behavior. In Thaler's view, "just as psychology has no unified theory … so behavioral economics will have a multitude of theories."[9] Ultimately, given that *Nudge* was published less than a decade ago, its long-term influence on mainstream economics remains to be seen.

NOTES

1   Cass R. Sunstein, "The Council of Psychological Advisers," *Forthcoming in Annual Review of Psychology*, accessed September 4, 2015, http://dash.harvard.edu/bitstream/handle/1/13031653/annualreview9_15.pdf?sequence=1.

2   Behavioural Insights Team, "Applying Behavioural Insights to Reduce Fraud, Error and Debt," February 2012, accessed September 4, 2015, https://www.gov.uk/government/uploads/system/uploads/attachment_data/file/60539/BIT_FraudErrorDebt_accessible.pdf.

3   Katrin Bennhold, "Britain's Ministry of Nudges," *New York Times*, December 7, 2013, accessed September 4, 2015, http://www.nytimes.com/2013/12/08/business/international/britains-ministry-of-nudges.html?_r=0.

4   Behavioural Insights Team, "Applying Behavioural Insights to Charitable Giving," accessed September 4, 2015, https://www.gov.uk/government/uploads/system/uploads/attachment_data/file/203286/BIT_Charitable_Giving_Paper.pdf.

5   Bennhold, "Britain's Ministry of Nudges."

6   Susan Michie et al., "The Behaviour Change Wheel: A New Method for Characterising and Designing Behaviour Change Interventions," *Implementation Science* 6, no. 42 (2011).

7   Morgan Housel, "Daniel Kahneman on Challenging Economic Assumptions," *Motley Fool*, June 29, 2013, accessed September 4, 2015, http://www.fool.com/investing/general/2013/06/29/challenging-assumptions-an-economist-considers-psy.aspx.

8   Colin F. Camerer and George Loewenstein, "Behavioral Economics: Past, Present, Future," in *Advances in Behavioral Economics*, ed. Colin F. Camerer et al. (Princeton, NJ: Princeton University Press, 2003).

9   Richard H. Thaler, "When Will There Be a Single Unified 'Behavioral' Theory of Economic Activity?" in "What's the Question about Your Field That You Dread Being Asked?" *Edge*, March 28, 2013, accessed September 4, 2015, http:/edge.org/conversation/whats-the-question-about-your-field-that-you-dread-being-asked#25056.

MODULE 12
WHERE NEXT?

KEY POINTS

- *Nudge* will likely continue to stimulate interest from academics and policymakers all over the world.
- The most significant long-term impact of *Nudge* may be to promote a norm of governance based on science.
- Bringing behavioral economics* to global prominence and promoting evidence-based policy-making has been the seminal contribution of *Nudge*.

Potential

Richard H. Thaler and Cass R. Sunstein's *Nudge: Improving Decisions about Health, Wealth, and Happiness* will likely continue to stimulate academic research in a diverse set of disciplines. It is a standard reference text on university courses in behavioral economics and has been cited by thousands of papers and reports. In the world of policy, the book's ideas have attracted interest from organizations as diverse as the World Bank,[*1] the OECD,[*2] the House of Lords (the upper chamber of the British Parliament),[3] and the governments of the United States, the United Kingdom, Germany, the Netherlands, Finland, Singapore, and Australia.[4] The list of policy areas *Nudge* has influenced is equally comprehensive, including tax collection, finance, immigration, charitable giving, energy efficiency and sustainability, criminality and fraud, unemployment, education, cybersecurity, and international development.[5]

Future Directions

In the long term, the most significant contributions of *Nudge* may be its promotion of two norms of science-based policy-making.

> **"**One of our main hopes is that an understanding of choice architecture, and the power of nudges, will lead others to think of creative ways to improve human lives in other domains. **"**
>
> Richard H. Thaler and Cass R. Sunstein, *Nudge: Improving Decisions about Health, Wealth, and Happiness*

The first is that policy-makers should use the best available science to design their interventions. This may mean using more than just the ideas in *Nudge*, which only suggests a relatively narrow spectrum of intervention types constrained by the principles of behavioral economics and libertarian paternalism.* This trend has already begun. The formal names of the UK and US Nudge Units do not use the words "nudge"* or "behavioral economics." They are called the Behavioural Insights Team* and the Social and Behavioral Sciences Team.* "Behavioral insights" and "social and behavioral sciences" are broad terms. These names allow these groups the freedom to use diverse sources of scientific evidence and different tools of intervention rather than just those discussed in *Nudge*.

The second norm is that policymakers should consistently test the effectiveness of their interventions using gold-standard scientific methods like randomized controlled trials,* or RCTs (a method used in the social sciences to determine the effectiveness of an intervention). This trend has already begun. In 2012 the UK Nudge Unit and a group of academics published "Test, Learn, Adapt," a report that argued UK policymakers should use RCTs to test the effectiveness of their interventions.[6] The Obama administration* in the US has also embraced RCTs, saying that government must use "rigorous evidence and evaluation to ensure that [it] makes smart investments with taxpayer funds."[7] Thaler, too, has spoken of the need to use RCTs in policy-making, saying that "you can't make evidence-based policy decisions without evidence."[8]

This norm is directly promoted by the Behavioural Insights Team in the UK and the Social and Behavioral Sciences Team in the US, whose annual reports meticulously document how their interventions are conducted and evaluated. The economist Justin Wolfers noted his approval of this trend in a *New York Times* commentary, saying that "the big idea is ... not about knowing how to do better, it's about testing what works. Experiment relentlessly, keep what works, and discard what doesn't. Following this recipe may yield a government that's ... clear, user-friendly and unflinchingly effective."[9]

While *Nudge* did not create either of these norms, its global success and emphasis on evidence-based policy has shone a spotlight on their importance.

Summary

Nudge made a convincing argument that governments could improve their citizens' lives without restricting their freedom of choice. It used evidence from behavioral economics and psychology to support this argument and gave specific, sensible suggestions on how policymakers could apply its ideas. Its global influence represents a major success for the field of behavioral economics and its theories of human decision-making.

The rise of behavioral economics mirrors the changing reputation of *Nudge* co-author Richard Thaler among mainstream economists. To quote the Harvard economist David Laibson,* "during most of the 1980s [Thaler] was dismissed as a crank ... It takes a lot of courage to get a decade of rejection and to stick to your guns. [Thaler] kept fighting, and eventually almost everyone came around to his view."[10] In 2015, Thaler became president of the American Economic Association, a sign of how his once-radical views have been accepted into mainstream economics.

NOTES

1 World Bank, "Mind, Society, and Behavior," *World Bank Group Flagship Report*, 2015, accessed September 26, 2015, http://www.worldbank.org/content/dam/Worldbank/Publications/WDR/WDR%202015/WDR-2015-Full-Report.pdf.

2 Pete Lunn, *Regulatory Policy and Behavioural Economics* (Paris: OECD Publishing, 2014).

3 House of Lords Science and Technology Select Committee, "Behaviour Change," *HL Paper* 179 (2011), accessed September 4, 2015, http://www.publications.parliament.uk/pa/ld201012/ldselect/ldsctech/179/179.pdf.

4 Behavioural Insights Team, "The Behavioural Insights Team Update Report 2013–2015," accessed September 4, 2015, http://www.behaviouralinsights.co.uk/wp-content/uploads/2015/07/BIT_Update-Report-Final-2013–2015.pdf.

5 Behavioural Insights Team, "Update Report 2013–2015."

6 Laura Haynes et al. "Test, Learn, Adapt: Developing Public Policy with Randomised Controlled Trials," *Cabinet Office*, June 2012, accessed September 4, 2015, https://www.gov.uk/government/uploads/system/uploads/attachment_data/file/62529/TLA-1906126.pdf.

7 Tom Kalil, "Funding What Works: The Importance of Low-Cost Randomized Controlled Trials," *White House Blog*, July 9, 2014, accessed September 4, 2015, https://www.whitehouse.gov/blog/2014/07/09/funding-what-works-importance-low-cost-randomized-controlled-trials.

8 Richard H. Thaler, "Watching Behavior before Writing the Rules," *New York Times*, July 7, 2012, accessed September 4, 2015, http://www.nytimes.com/2012/07/08/business/behavioral-science-can-help-guide-policy-economic-view.html.

9 Justin Wolfers, "A Better Government, One Tweak at a Time," *New York Times*, September 25, 2015, accessed September 30, 2015, http://www.nytimes.com/2015/09/27/upshot/a-better-government-one-tweak-at-a-time.html?rref=upshot&_r=0.

10 Gregory Karp, "Profile: Richard Thaler, University of Chicago Booth School of Business Professor," *Chicago Tribune*, April 30, 2012, accessed September 4, 2015, http://articles.chicagotribune.com/2012–04-30/business/ct-biz-0430–executive-profile-thaler-20120430_1_economics-daniel-kahneman-cost-fallacy.

GLOSSARY

GLOSSARY OF TERMS

"Anomalies": the title of Richard Thaler's influential column in the *Journal of Economic Perspectives* during the 1980s and 1990s. He used this column as a platform to introduce the ideas of behavioral economics to a mainstream economic audience.

Automatic and Reflective systems: a theory based on research in psychology and neuroscience that conceives of two distinct types of human thinking: the fast and instinctive Automatic System, and the more ponderous and calculating Reflective System.

Availability heuristic: a mental rule-of-thumb according to which people use examples that come readily to mind when making a judgment.

Behavioral economics: a subdiscipline of economics that integrates findings from psychology into models of economic decision-making.

Behavioral science: a broad term that includes the ideas of behavioral economics, psychology, and other academic disciplines that contribute to an understanding of human behavior.

Behavioural Insights Team: an influential group established in the United Kingdom by Prime Minister David Cameron in 2010 to implement the ideas of *Nudge* within government.

Chicago school: a neoclassical economic school of thought that is associated with the University of Chicago economics department.

Choice architecture: the context in which people make decisions.

Cognitive bias: a way of interpreting the world that can cause systematic deviations from rational judgments and behavior.

Conservative party: a right-wing political party in the United Kingdom, founded in 1834.

Constitutional law: a body of law derived from a country's written constitution.

Consumer Financial Protection Agency: a US government agency established in 2011, responsible for consumer protection in the finance sector.

Democratic party: one of the two main political parties in the United States. Founded in 1828, it is associated with center–left politics.

Econometrica: one of the most prestigious journals in the field of economics, in publication since 1933.

Econs and Humans: the terms Thaler and Sunstein used to distinguish between ideal decision-makers in economic models (Econs) and people who make decisions in the real world (Humans).

Financial Conduct Authority: a regulatory body in the United Kingdom that monitors the financial services industry.

Heuristic: a mental rule-of-thumb used in decision-making.

Journal of Economic Perspectives: an economic journal covering a broad range of topics, in publication since 1987.

Judicial minimalism: a philosophy that advocates incremental interpretations of American constitutional law.

Labour party: a center–left political party in the United Kingdom.

Libertarianism: a political philosophy that emphasizes individual liberty and freedom of choice.

Libertarian paternalism: the philosophy discussed in *Nudge*. Thaler and Sunstein describe it as a "soft" paternalism that encourages people to act in their own best interest without restricting their freedom of choice.

Loss aversion: the tendency for people to favor avoiding loss over receiving gain.

Neoclassical economics: the mainstream synthesis of economic thought developed after World War II. It assumes a model of human behavior in which people have rational preferences and act on the basis of complete information.

Nudge: any aspect of choice architecture that changes people's behavior in a predictable way, and is cheap and easy to avoid.

Nudge Unit: the informal name of the Behavioural Insights Team.

Obama administration: the government of US President Barack Obama, in office since January 2009 and scheduled to remain in power until January 2017.

OECD: the Organization for Economic Co-operation and Development, a group of countries that promote democracy and economic growth via the market economy system.

Paternalism: a type of behavior by an individual or group that restricts a person's freedom of choice for what is judged to be their own good.

"Prospect Theory": the title of a seminal paper in behavioral economics, published by Daniel Kahneman and Amos Tversky in *Econometrica* in 1979.

Randomized controlled trial (RCT): the gold-standard methodology used in the social sciences to evaluate the effectiveness of an intervention.

Rational actor: a person who behaves according to the assumptions of rational choice theory.

Rational choice theory: the main framework used in neoclassical economics for understanding human behavior in social and economic contexts.

"Regulation for Conservatives": the title of a 2003 paper by the behavioral economist Colin Camerer and colleagues. It introduced the philosophy of "asymmetric paternalism," which is very similar to *Nudge*'s "libertarian paternalism."

Republican party: one of the two main political parties in the United States. Founded in 1854, it is associated with right-wing politics.

Science: one of the world's most prestigious scientific journals, in publication since 1880.

Social and Behavioral Sciences Team: a group formally established by executive order of President Barack Obama in 2015 to promote the use of behavioral science in the US government.

The Theory of Moral Sentiments: a book by the Scottish philosopher Adam Smith published in 1759, considered to be the foundational text of the field of behavioral economics.

Third way: a term for a political position, used by many different politicians during the twentieth century, that attempts to reconcile differences in right- and left-wing political ideology by adopting policies from both points of view. Thaler and Sunstein argue that the policy ideas in *Nudge* represent a "real third way."

2008 financial crisis: a period of economic recession considered to be the worst in the developed world since the Great Depression of the 1930s.

World Bank: an international organization designed to reduce global poverty by providing loans to developing countries for infrastructural development.

World War II: the global conflict that took place between 1939 and 1945 between Germany, Italy, and Japan (the Axis powers) and Britain, the Soviet Union, the United States, and other nations (the Allies). One of the defining events of the twentieth century.

PEOPLE MENTIONED IN THE TEXT

John Beshears is a professor of business administration at Harvard Business School. His research applies behavioral economics to individual decision-making and market outcomes.

Luc Bovens (b. 1961) is a Belgian professor of philosophy at the London School of Economics who has written on the ethics of nudging.

Colin Camerer (b. 1959) is an American behavioral economist and professor of behavioral finance and economics at the California Institute of Technology. He is part of a group of academics who developed the concept of "asymmetric paternalism," a similar philosophy to "libertarian paternalism."

David Cameron (b. 1966) is the current prime minister of the United Kingdom, in office since 2010.

Werner De Bondt is a Belgian economist who has collaborated with Richard Thaler in the field of behavioral finance.

Milton Friedman (1912–2006) was the winner of the Nobel Prize in Economics in 1976 and one of the most influential economists of the twentieth century. He is strongly associated with the Chicago school of economic thought.

David Halpern is a British psychologist, director of the Behavioural Insights Team, also known as the Nudge Unit.

Christine Jolls (b. 1967) is an American law professor at Yale Law School who has written on the applications of behavioral economics to matters of law.

Daniel Kahneman (b. 1934) is an Israeli psychologist, winner of the Nobel Prize in Economics in 2002 for his work on decision-making with Amos Tversky, and professor emeritus of psychology and public affairs at Princeton University.

David Laibson (b. 1966) is an American behavioral economist and professor of economics at Harvard University. He has written several influential papers applying the idea of limited self-control to economic behavior.

George Loewenstein (b. 1955) is an American behavioral economist and professor of economics and psychology at Carnegie Mellon University. He coauthored with Colin Camerer an influential text describing the history of behavioral economics.

Pete Lunn is an Irish economist who has written on the applications of behavioral economics to matters of regulation and public policy.

Brigitte Madrian is an American professor of public policy at the Harvard Kennedy School of Harvard University. In 2000 she wrote an influential article with Dennis Shea that demonstrated the importance of default rules in pension-enrollment programs.

Susan Michie (b. 1955) is a British professor of health psychology at University College London. She has criticized the limits of nudging for health interventions and developed an alternative framework called the Behaviour Change Wheel.

Ed Miliband (b. 1969) is a British politician and former leader of the Labour party between 2010 and 2015.

Baroness Julia Neuberger (b. 1950) is a member of the House of Lords (the upper chamber of the British Parliament). She headed that institution's 2011 report on behavior change, which examined the efficacy of nudging.

Barack Obama (b. 1961) is the 44th president of the United States, elected in 2009 and scheduled to serve until 2017.

George Osborne (b. 1971) is first secretary of state and chancellor of the exchequer of the United Kingdom.

Richard Posner (b. 1939) is an American legal scholar, economist, and noted critic of behavioral economics.

Barry Schwartz (b. 1946) is an American psychologist who has written on the psychology of human decision-making.

Dennis Shea was the vice-president of American health care company UnitedHealth Group in 2000. He conducted a study on pension auto-enrollment with Brigitte Madrian.

Herbert Simon (1916–2001) was an American academic and winner of the Nobel Prize in Economics in 1978. He introduced the concept of "bounded rationality" as a basis for understanding human decision-making.

Adam Smith (1723–90) was a Scottish philosopher who is considered a founding figure of the fields of economics and behavioral economics for his books *The Wealth of Nations* and *The Theory of Moral Sentiments*.

Amos Tversky (1937–96) was an Israeli psychologist known for his work with Daniel Kahneman on human decision-making.

WORKS CITED

WORKS CITED

Anderson, Joel. "Review of *Nudge: Improving Decisions and Health, Wealth, and Happiness.*" *Economics and Philosophy* 26, no. 3 (2010): 369–76.

Becker, Gary. "Irrational Behavior and Economic Theory." *Journal of Political Economy* 70, no. 1 (1962): 1–13.

"Behavioural Finance to the Rescue?" *Economist*, August 18, 2009. Accessed September 26, 2015. http://www.economist.com/blogs/freeexchange/2009/08/behavioural_finance_to_the_res.

Behavioural Insights Team. "Applying Behavioural Insights to Charitable Giving." Accessed September 4, 2015. https://www.gov.uk/government/uploads/system/uploads/attachment_data/file/203286/BIT_Charitable_Giving_Paper.pdf.

"Applying Behavioural Insights to Reduce Fraud, Error and Debt." February 2012. Accessed September 4, 2015. https://www.gov.uk/government/uploads/system/uploads/attachment_data/file/60539/BIT_FraudErrorDebt_accessible.pdf.

"Behavioural Exchange 2014." Accessed September 30, 2015. http://www.behaviouralinsights.co.uk/bx2015/behavioural-exchange-2014/.

"The Behavioural Insights Team Update Report 2013–2015." Accessed September 4, 2015. http://www.behaviouralinsights.co.uk/wp-content/uploads/2015/07/BIT_Update-Report-Final-2013–2015.pdf.

"Who We Are." Accessed September 4, 2015. http://www.behaviouralinsights.co.uk/about-us/.

Bennhold, Katrin. "Britain's Ministry of Nudges." *New York Times*, December 7, 2013. Accessed September 4, 2015. http://www.nytimes.com/2013/12/08/business/international/britains-ministry-of-nudges.html?_r=0.

Beshears, John, James J. Choi, David Laibson, and Brigitte C. Madrian. "How Are Preferences Revealed?" *Journal of Public Economics* 92 (2008): 1787–94.

"Best Business Books." *Financial Times*, 2008. Accessed September 4, 2015. http://ig.ft.com/sites/business-book-award/books/2008/longlist/nudge-by-richard-thaler-and-cass-sunstein.

Bovens, Luc. "The Ethics of Nudge." In *Preference Change: Approaches from Philosophy, Economics and Psychology*, edited by Till Grüne-Yanoff and Sven Ove Hansson, 207–19. New York: Springer, 2009.

Camerer, Colin F., and George Loewenstein. "Behavioral Economics: Past, Present, Future." In *Advances in Behavioral Economics*, edited by Colin F. Camerer, George Loewenstein, and Matthew Rabin. Princeton, NJ: Princeton University Press, 2003.

Camerer, Colin F., Samuel Issacharoff, George Loewenstein, Ted O'Donoghue, and Matthew Rabin. "Regulation for Conservatives: Behavioral Economics and the Case for 'Asymmetric Paternalism.'" *University of Pennsylvania Law Review* 151, no. 3 (2003): 1211–54.

Cameron, David. "The Next Age of Government." *TED*, February 2010. Accessed September 4, 2015. http://www.ted.com/talks/david_cameron?language=en.

Cassidy, John. "After the Blowup." *New Yorker*, January 11, 2010. Accessed September 26, 2015. http://www.newyorker.com/magazine/2010/01/11/after-the-blowup.

Clement, Douglas. "Interview with Richard Thaler." *The Region Magazine*, October 3, 2013. Accessed September 4, 2015. https://www.minneapolisfed.org/publications/the-region/interview-with-richard-thaler.

Day, Elizabeth. "Julia Neuberger: 'A Nudge in the Right Direction Won't Run the Big Society.'" *Observer*, July 17, 2011. Accessed September 4, 2015. http://www.theguardian.com/society/2011/jul/17/julia-neuberger-nudge-big-society.

De Bondt, Werner F. M., and Richard H. Thaler. "Does the Stock Market Overreact?" *Journal of Finance* 40, no. 3 (1985): 793–805.

Erta, Kristine, Stefan Hunt, Zanna Iscenko, and Will Brambley. "Applying Behavioural Economics at the Financial Conduct Authority." *FCA Occasional Paper* no. 1 (2013). Accessed September 4, 2015. https://www.fca.org.uk/static/documents/occasional-papers/occasional-paper-1.pdf.

"Executive Summary of Financial Regulatory Reform: A New Foundation." *US Treasury Department*, June 17, 2009. Accessed September 4, 2015. http://www.treasury.gov/initiatives/wsr/Documents/executive_summary.pdf.

Friedman, Benjamin M. "Guiding Forces." *New York Times*, August 22, 2008. Accessed September 5, 2015. http://www.nytimes.com/2008/08/24/books/review/Friedman-t.html?pagewanted=all&_r=0.

FT View, "Economics Needs to Reflect a Post-Crisis World." *Financial Times*, September 25, 2014. Accessed October 15, 2015. http://www.ft.com/cms/s/0/f9f65e88-44a3-11e4-ab0c-00144feabdc0.html#axzz3ojq0z1zz.

Goldstein, Daniel G., Eric J. Johnson, Andreas Herrmann, and Mark Heitmann. "Nudge Your Customers toward Better Choices." *Harvard Business Review*, December 2008. Accessed September 4, 2015. https://hbr.org/2008/12/nudge-your-customers-toward-better-choices.

Goodwin, Neva, Jonathan Harris, Julie A. Nelson, Brian Roach, and Mariano Torras. *Microeconomics in Context*. 3rd edn. Abingdon: Routledge, 2013.

Google Scholar. List of texts that have cited *Nudge* as of September 26, 2015. Accessed October 15, 2015. https://scholar.google.com/scholar?cites=16854468477297806637&as_sdt=2005&sciodt=0,5&hl=en.

Halonen, Elina. "Research Heroes: Richard Thaler." *InDecision Blog*, January 15, 2013. Accessed September 4, 2015. http://indecisionblog.com/2013/01/15/research-heroes-richard-thaler/.

Haynes, Laura, Owain Service, Ben Goldacre, and David Torgerson. "Test, Learn, Adapt: Developing Public Policy with Randomised Controlled Trials." *Cabinet Office*, 2012. Accessed September 4, 2015. https://www.gov.uk/government/uploads/system/uploads/attachment_data/file/62529/TLA-1906126.pdf.

House of Lords Science and Technology Select Committee. "Behaviour Change Report." *HL Paper* 179 (2011). Accessed September 4, 2015. http://www.publications.parliament.uk/pa/ld201012/ldselect/ldsctech/179/179.pdf.

Housel, Morgan. "Daniel Kahneman on Challenging Economic Assumptions." *Motley Fool*, June 29, 2013. Accessed September 4, 2015. http://www.fool.com/investing/general/2013/06/29/challenging-assumptions-an-economist-considers-psy.aspx.

Jolls, Christine, Cass R. Sunstein, and Richard H. Thaler. "A Behavioral Approach to Law and Economics." *Stanford Law Review* 50, no. 5 (1998): 1471–550.

Kahneman, Daniel. *Thinking, Fast and Slow*. New York: Farrar, Straus and Giroux, 2011.

Kahneman, Daniel, and Amos Tversky. "Prospect Theory: An Analysis of Decision under Risk." *Econometrica* 47, no. 2 (1979): 263–92.

Kalil, Tom. "Funding What Works: The Importance of Low-Cost Randomized Controlled Trials." *White House Blog*, July 9, 2014. Accessed September 4, 2015. https://www.whitehouse.gov/blog/2014/07/09/funding-what-works-importance-low-cost-randomized-controlled-trials.

Karp, Gregory. "Profile: Richard Thaler, University of Chicago Booth School of Business Professor." *Chicago Tribune*, April 30, 2012. Accessed September 4, 2015. http://articles.chicagotribune.com/2012–04-30/business/ct-biz-0430–executive-profile-thaler-20120430_1_economics-daniel-kahneman-cost-fallacy.

Krugman, Paul. "How Did Economists Get It So Wrong?" *New York Times*, September 6, 2009. Accessed September 26, 2015. http://www.econ.ucdavis.edu/faculty/kdsalyer/LECTURES/Ecn200e/krugman_macro.pdf.

Kuang, Cliff. "In the Cafeteria, Google Gets Healthy." *Fast Company Magazine*, March 19, 2012. Accessed September 4, 2015. http://www.fastcompany.com/1822516/cafeteria-google-gets-healthy.

Laibson, David. "Golden Eggs and Hyperbolic Discounting." *Quarterly Journal of Economics* 112 no. 2 (1997): 443–78.

Leonard, Thomas C. "Richard H. Thaler, Cass R. Sunstein, 'Nudge: Improving Decisions about Health, Wealth, and Happiness.'" *Constitutional Political Economy Book Review*, 2008. Accessed September 4, 2015. http://www. princeton.edu/~tleonard/reviews/nudge.pdf.

Lunn, Pete. *Regulatory Policy and Behavioural Economics*. Paris: OECD Publishing, 2014.

Madrian, Brigitte C., and Dennis F. Shea. "The Power of Suggestion: Inertia in 401(k) Participation and Savings Behavior." *Quarterly Journal of Economics* 116, no. 4 (2001): 1149–87.

Marteau, Theresa M., David Ogilvie, Martin Roland, Marc Suhrcke, and Michael P. Kelly. "Judging Nudging: Can Nudging Improve Population Health?" *British Medical Journal* 342 (2011).

Michie, Susan, Maartje M. van Stralen, and Robert West. "The Behaviour Change Wheel: A New Method for Characterising and Designing Behaviour Change Interventions." *Implementation Science* 6, no. 42 (2011).

Nickerson, David W., and Todd Rogers. "Do You Have a Voting Plan? Implementation Intentions, Voter Turnout, and Organic Plan Making." *Psychological Science* 21, no. 2 (2010): 194–9.

Orwid, John. "Behavioral Economics Gives the Advertising Industry a Nudge in the Right Direction." *Forbes*, February 5, 2014. Accessed September 26, 2015. http://www.forbes.com/sites/johnowrid/2014/02/05/behavioural-economics-gives-the-advertising-industry-a-nudge-in-the-right-direction/.

Osborne, George. "Nudge, Nudge, Win, Win." *Guardian*, July 14, 2008. Accessed September 4, 2015. http://www.theguardian.com/ commentisfree/2008/jul/14/conservatives.economy.

"Pick of the Pile." *Economist*, December 4, 2008. Accessed September 4, 2015. http://www.economist.com/node/12719711.

Posner, Richard A. "Treating Financial Consumers as Consenting Adults." *Wall Street Journal*, July 22, 2009. Accessed September 4, 2015. http://www.wsj. com/articles/SB10001424052970203946904574302213213148166.

Schnellenbach, Jan, and Christian Schubert. "Behavioral Political Economy: A Survey." *European Journal of Political Economy*, in press (2015).

Schwartz, Barry. "Why Not Nudge? A Review of Cass Sunstein's *Why Nudge?*" *thepsychreport,* April 17, 2014. Accessed September 4, 2015. http:// thepsychreport.com/essays-discussion/nudge-review-cass-sunsteins-why-nudge/.

Shafir, Eldar (ed.). *The Behavioral Foundations of Public Policy*. Princeton, NJ: Princeton University Press, 2012.

Smith, Noah. "Five Economists Who Deserve Nobels." *Bloomberg View*, December 9, 2014. Accessed September 4, 2015. http://www.bloombergview. com/articles/2014-12–09/five-economists-who-deserve-nobels.

Social and Behavioral Sciences Team. "Social and Behavioral Sciences Team Annual Report." *Executive Office of the President National Science and Technology Council*, September 2015. Accessed September 30, 2015. https://www.whitehouse.gov/sites/default/files/microsites/ostp/sbst_2015_annual_report_final_9_14_15.pdf.

Sparrow, Andrew. "Fabian Conference—Live." *Guardian*, January 17, 2009. Accessed September 4, 2015. http://www.theguardian.com/politics/blog/2009/jan/17/fabian-conference-blog.

Sunstein, Cass R. "The Council of Psychological Advisers." *Forthcoming in Annual Review of Psychology*. Accessed September 4, 2015. http://dash.harvard.edu/bitstream/handle/1/13031653/annualreview9_15.pdf?sequence=1.

"Nudges: Good and Bad." *New York Review of Books*, October 23, 2014. Accessed September 4, 2015. http://www.nybooks.com/articles/archives/2014/oct/23/nudges-good-and-bad/.

Simpler: The Future of Government. New York: Simon & Schuster, 2013.

"There's a Backlash against Nudging—But It Was Never Meant to Solve Every Problem." *Guardian*, April 24, 2014. Accessed September 4, 2015. http://www.theguardian.com/commentisfree/2014/apr/24/nudge-backlash-free-society-dignity-coercion.

Why Nudge? New York: Yale University Press, 2014.

"Sveriges Riksbank Prize in Economic Sciences in Memory of Alfred Nobel, 2002." *Nobelprize.org*. Accessed September 4, 2015. http://www.nobelprize.org/nobel_prizes/economic-sciences/laureates/2002/.

Thaler, Richard H. "Anomalies." Accessed September 4, 2015. http://faculty.chicagobooth.edu/Richard.Thaler/research/anomalies.html.

"Do You Need a Nudge?" *Yale Insights*, November 4, 2009. Accessed September 4, 2015. http://insights.som.yale.edu/insights/do-you-need-nudge.

"Thaler Responds to Posner on Consumer Protection." *PBS Newshour*, July 28, 2009. Accessed September 4, 2015. http://www.pbs.org/newshour/making-sense/thaler-responds-to-posner-on-c/.

"Watching Behavior before Writing the Rules." *New York Times*, July 7, 2012. Accessed September 4, 2015. http://www.nytimes.com/2012/07/08/business/behavioral-science-can-help-guide-policy-economic-view.html.

"When Will There Be a Single Unified 'Behavioral' Theory of Economic Activity?" in "What's the Question about Your Field That You Dread Being Asked?" *Edge*, March 28, 2013. Accessed September 4, 2015. http://edge.org/conversation/whats-the-question-about-your-field-that-you-dread-being-asked#25056.

Thaler, Richard H., and Cass R. Sunstein. "Libertarian Paternalism Is Not an Oxymoron." *University of Chicago Law Review* 70, no. 4 (2003): 1159-1202.

"Libertarian Paternalism." *The American Economic Review* 93, no. 2 (2003): 175–9.

Nudge: Improving Decisions about Health, Wealth, and Happiness. New York: Yale University Press, 2008.

Tversky, Amos, and Daniel Kahneman. "Judgment under Uncertainty: Heuristics and Biases." *Science* 185, no. 4157 (1974): 1124–31.

Ubel, Peter. "Q & A with Richard Thaler on What It Really Means to Be a 'Nudge.'" *Forbes*, February 20, 2015. Accessed September 4, 2015. http://www.forbes.com/sites/peterubel/2015/02/20/q-a-with-richard-thaler-on-what-it-really-means-to-be-a-nudge/.

Varian, Hal. *Intermediate Microeconomics*. 8th edn. New York: W. W. Norton & Company, 2009.

Waldron, Jeremy. "It's All for Your Own Good." *New York Review of Books*, October 9, 2014. Accessed September 4, 2015. http://www.nybooks.com/articles/archives/2014/oct/09/cass-sunstein-its-all-your-own-good/.

White House. "Executive Order—Using Behavioral Science Insights to Better Serve the American People." *Office of the Press Secretary*, September 15, 2015. Accessed September 30, 2015. https://www.whitehouse.gov/the-press-office/2015/09/15/executive-order-using-behavioral-science-insights-better-serve-american.

Wolfers, Justin. "A Better Government, One Tweak at a Time." *New York Times*, September 25, 2015. Accessed September 30, 2015. http://www.nytimes.com/2015/09/27/upshot/a-better-government-one-tweak-at-a-time.html?rref=upshot&_r=0.

World Bank. "Mind, Society, and Behavior," *World Bank Group Flagship Report*, 2015. Accessed September 26, 2015. www.worldbank.org/content/dam/Worldbank/Publications/WDR/WDR%202015/WDR-2015-Full-Report.pdf

Zipkin, Nina. "Attention, Apple Shoppers: You're Being Followed." December 6, 2013. Accessed September 4, 2015. http://www.entrepreneur.com/article/230275.

THE MACAT LIBRARY
BY DISCIPLINE

AFRICANA STUDIES

Chinua Achebe's *An Image of Africa: Racism in Conrad's Heart of Darkness*
W. E. B. Du Bois's *The Souls of Black Folk*
Zora Neale Huston's *Characteristics of Negro Expression*
Martin Luther King Jr's *Why We Can't Wait*
Toni Morrison's *Playing in the Dark: Whiteness in the American Literary Imagination*

ANTHROPOLOGY

Arjun Appadurai's *Modernity at Large: Cultural Dimensions of Globalisation*
Philippe Ariès's *Centuries of Childhood*
Franz Boas's *Race, Language and Culture*
Kim Chan & Renée Mauborgne's *Blue Ocean Strategy*
Jared Diamond's *Guns, Germs & Steel: the Fate of Human Societies*
Jared Diamond's *Collapse: How Societies Choose to Fail or Survive*
E. E. Evans-Pritchard's *Witchcraft, Oracles and Magic Among the Azande*
James Ferguson's *The Anti-Politics Machine*
Clifford Geertz's *The Interpretation of Cultures*
David Graeber's *Debt: the First 5000 Years*
Karen Ho's *Liquidated: An Ethnography of Wall Street*
Geert Hofstede's *Culture's Consequences: Comparing Values, Behaviors, Institutes and Organizations across Nations*
Claude Lévi-Strauss's *Structural Anthropology*
Jay Macleod's *Ain't No Makin' It: Aspirations and Attainment in a Low-Income Neighborhood*
Saba Mahmood's *The Politics of Piety: The Islamic Revival and the Feminist Subject*
Marcel Mauss's *The Gift*

BUSINESS

Jean Lave & Etienne Wenger's *Situated Learning*
Theodore Levitt's *Marketing Myopia*
Burton G. Malkiel's *A Random Walk Down Wall Street*
Douglas McGregor's *The Human Side of Enterprise*
Michael Porter's *Competitive Strategy: Creating and Sustaining Superior Performance*
John Kotter's *Leading Change*
C. K. Prahalad & Gary Hamel's *The Core Competence of the Corporation*

CRIMINOLOGY

Michelle Alexander's *The New Jim Crow: Mass Incarceration in the Age of Colorblindness*
Michael R. Gottfredson & Travis Hirschi's *A General Theory of Crime*
Richard Herrnstein & Charles A. Murray's *The Bell Curve: Intelligence and Class Structure in American Life*
Elizabeth Loftus's *Eyewitness Testimony*
Jay Macleod's *Ain't No Makin' It: Aspirations and Attainment in a Low-Income Neighborhood*
Philip Zimbardo's *The Lucifer Effect*

ECONOMICS

Janet Abu-Lughod's *Before European Hegemony*
Ha-Joon Chang's *Kicking Away the Ladder*
David Brion Davis's *The Problem of Slavery in the Age of Revolution*
Milton Friedman's *The Role of Monetary Policy*
Milton Friedman's *Capitalism and Freedom*
David Graeber's *Debt: the First 5000 Years*
Friedrich Hayek's *The Road to Serfdom*
Karen Ho's *Liquidated: An Ethnography of Wall Street*

John Maynard Keynes's *The General Theory of Employment, Interest and Money*
Charles P. Kindleberger's *Manias, Panics and Crashes*
Robert Lucas's *Why Doesn't Capital Flow from Rich to Poor Countries?*
Burton G. Malkiel's *A Random Walk Down Wall Street*
Thomas Robert Malthus's *An Essay on the Principle of Population*
Karl Marx's *Capital*
Thomas Piketty's *Capital in the Twenty-First Century*
Amartya Sen's *Development as Freedom*
Adam Smith's *The Wealth of Nations*
Nassim Nicholas Taleb's *The Black Swan: The Impact of the Highly Improbable*
Amos Tversky's & Daniel Kahneman's *Judgment under Uncertainty: Heuristics and Biases*
Mahbub Ul Haq's *Reflections on Human Development*
Max Weber's *The Protestant Ethic and the Spirit of Capitalism*

FEMINISM AND GENDER STUDIES

Judith Butler's *Gender Trouble*
Simone De Beauvoir's *The Second Sex*
Michel Foucault's *History of Sexuality*
Betty Friedan's *The Feminine Mystique*
Saba Mahmood's *The Politics of Piety: The Islamic Revival and the Feminist Subject*
Joan Wallach Scott's *Gender and the Politics of History*
Mary Wollstonecraft's *A Vindication of the Rights of Women*
Virginia Woolf's *A Room of One's Own*

GEOGRAPHY

The Brundtland Report's *Our Common Future*
Rachel Carson's *Silent Spring*
Charles Darwin's *On the Origin of Species*
James Ferguson's *The Anti-Politics Machine*
Jane Jacobs's *The Death and Life of Great American Cities*
James Lovelock's *Gaia: A New Look at Life on Earth*
Amartya Sen's *Development as Freedom*
Mathis Wackernagel & William Rees's *Our Ecological Footprint*

HISTORY

Janet Abu-Lughod's *Before European Hegemony*
Benedict Anderson's *Imagined Communities*
Bernard Bailyn's *The Ideological Origins of the American Revolution*
Hanna Batatu's *The Old Social Classes And The Revolutionary Movements Of Iraq*
Christopher Browning's *Ordinary Men: Reserve Police Batallion 101 and the Final Solution in Poland*
Edmund Burke's *Reflections on the Revolution in France*
William Cronon's *Nature's Metropolis: Chicago And The Great West*
Alfred W. Crosby's *The Columbian Exchange*
Hamid Dabashi's *Iran: A People Interrupted*
David Brion Davis's *The Problem of Slavery in the Age of Revolution*
Nathalie Zemon Davis's *The Return of Martin Guerre*
Jared Diamond's *Guns, Germs & Steel: the Fate of Human Societies*
Frank Dikotter's *Mao's Great Famine*
John W Dower's *War Without Mercy: Race And Power In The Pacific War*
W. E. B. Du Bois's *The Souls of Black Folk*
Richard J. Evans's *In Defence of History*
Lucien Febvre's *The Problem of Unbelief in the 16th Century*
Sheila Fitzpatrick's *Everyday Stalinism*

Eric Foner's *Reconstruction: America's Unfinished Revolution, 1863-1877*
Michel Foucault's *Discipline and Punish*
Michel Foucault's *History of Sexuality*
Francis Fukuyama's *The End of History and the Last Man*
John Lewis Gaddis's *We Now Know: Rethinking Cold War History*
Ernest Gellner's *Nations and Nationalism*
Eugene Genovese's *Roll, Jordan, Roll: The World the Slaves Made*
Carlo Ginzburg's *The Night Battles*
Daniel Goldhagen's *Hitler's Willing Executioners*
Jack Goldstone's *Revolution and Rebellion in the Early Modern World*
Antonio Gramsci's *The Prison Notebooks*
Alexander Hamilton, John Jay & James Madison's *The Federalist Papers*
Christopher Hill's *The World Turned Upside Down*
Carole Hillenbrand's *The Crusades: Islamic Perspectives*
Thomas Hobbes's *Leviathan*
Eric Hobsbawm's *The Age Of Revolution*
John A. Hobson's *Imperialism: A Study*
Albert Hourani's *History of the Arab Peoples*
Samuel P. Huntington's *The Clash of Civilizations and the Remaking of World Order*
C. L. R. James's *The Black Jacobins*
Tony Judt's *Postwar: A History of Europe Since 1945*
Ernst Kantorowicz's *The King's Two Bodies: A Study in Medieval Political Theology*
Paul Kennedy's *The Rise and Fall of the Great Powers*
Ian Kershaw's *The "Hitler Myth": Image and Reality in the Third Reich*
John Maynard Keynes's *The General Theory of Employment, Interest and Money*
Charles P. Kindleberger's *Manias, Panics and Crashes*
Martin Luther King Jr's *Why We Can't Wait*
Henry Kissinger's *World Order: Reflections on the Character of Nations and the Course of History*
Thomas Kuhn's *The Structure of Scientific Revolutions*
Georges Lefebvre's *The Coming of the French Revolution*
John Locke's *Two Treatises of Government*
Niccolò Machiavelli's *The Prince*
Thomas Robert Malthus's *An Essay on the Principle of Population*
Mahmood Mamdani's *Citizen and Subject: Contemporary Africa And The Legacy Of Late Colonialism*
Karl Marx's *Capital*
Stanley Milgram's *Obedience to Authority*
John Stuart Mill's *On Liberty*
Thomas Paine's *Common Sense*
Thomas Paine's *Rights of Man*
Geoffrey Parker's *Global Crisis: War, Climate Change and Catastrophe in the Seventeenth Century*
Jonathan Riley-Smith's *The First Crusade and the Idea of Crusading*
Jean-Jacques Rousseau's *The Social Contract*
Joan Wallach Scott's *Gender and the Politics of History*
Theda Skocpol's *States and Social Revolutions*
Adam Smith's *The Wealth of Nations*
Timothy Snyder's *Bloodlands: Europe Between Hitler and Stalin*
Sun Tzu's *The Art of War*
Keith Thomas's *Religion and the Decline of Magic*
Thucydides's *The History of the Peloponnesian War*
Frederick Jackson Turner's *The Significance of the Frontier in American History*
Odd Arne Westad's *The Global Cold War: Third World Interventions And The Making Of Our Times*

LITERATURE

Chinua Achebe's *An Image of Africa: Racism in Conrad's Heart of Darkness*
Roland Barthes's *Mythologies*
Homi K. Bhabha's *The Location of Culture*
Judith Butler's *Gender Trouble*
Simone De Beauvoir's *The Second Sex*
Ferdinand De Saussure's *Course in General Linguistics*
T. S. Eliot's *The Sacred Wood: Essays on Poetry and Criticism*
Zora Neale Huston's *Characteristics of Negro Expression*
Toni Morrison's *Playing in the Dark: Whiteness in the American Literary Imagination*
Edward Said's *Orientalism*
Gayatri Chakravorty Spivak's *Can the Subaltern Speak?*
Mary Wollstonecraft's *A Vindication of the Rights of Women*
Virginia Woolf's *A Room of One's Own*

PHILOSOPHY

Elizabeth Anscombe's *Modern Moral Philosophy*
Hannah Arendt's *The Human Condition*
Aristotle's *Metaphysics*
Aristotle's *Nicomachean Ethics*
Edmund Gettier's *Is Justified True Belief Knowledge?*
Georg Wilhelm Friedrich Hegel's *Phenomenology of Spirit*
David Hume's *Dialogues Concerning Natural Religion*
David Hume's *The Enquiry for Human Understanding*
Immanuel Kant's *Religion within the Boundaries of Mere Reason*
Immanuel Kant's *Critique of Pure Reason*
Søren Kierkegaard's *The Sickness Unto Death*
Søren Kierkegaard's *Fear and Trembling*
C. S. Lewis's *The Abolition of Man*
Alasdair MacIntyre's *After Virtue*
Marcus Aurelius's *Meditations*
Friedrich Nietzsche's *On the Genealogy of Morality*
Friedrich Nietzsche's *Beyond Good and Evil*
Plato's *Republic*
Plato's *Symposium*
Jean-Jacques Rousseau's *The Social Contract*
Gilbert Ryle's *The Concept of Mind*
Baruch Spinoza's *Ethics*
Sun Tzu's *The Art of War*
Ludwig Wittgenstein's *Philosophical Investigations*

POLITICS

Benedict Anderson's *Imagined Communities*
Aristotle's *Politics*
Bernard Bailyn's *The Ideological Origins of the American Revolution*
Edmund Burke's *Reflections on the Revolution in France*
John C. Calhoun's *A Disquisition on Government*
Ha-Joon Chang's *Kicking Away the Ladder*
Hamid Dabashi's *Iran: A People Interrupted*
Hamid Dabashi's *Theology of Discontent: The Ideological Foundation of the Islamic Revolution in Iran*
Robert Dahl's *Democracy and its Critics*
Robert Dahl's *Who Governs?*
David Brion Davis's *The Problem of Slavery in the Age of Revolution*

Alexis De Tocqueville's *Democracy in America*
James Ferguson's *The Anti-Politics Machine*
Frank Dikotter's *Mao's Great Famine*
Sheila Fitzpatrick's *Everyday Stalinism*
Eric Foner's *Reconstruction: America's Unfinished Revolution, 1863-1877*
Milton Friedman's *Capitalism and Freedom*
Francis Fukuyama's *The End of History and the Last Man*
John Lewis Gaddis's *We Now Know: Rethinking Cold War History*
Ernest Gellner's *Nations and Nationalism*
David Graeber's *Debt: the First 5000 Years*
Antonio Gramsci's *The Prison Notebooks*
Alexander Hamilton, John Jay & James Madison's *The Federalist Papers*
Friedrich Hayek's *The Road to Serfdom*
Christopher Hill's *The World Turned Upside Down*
Thomas Hobbes's *Leviathan*
John A. Hobson's *Imperialism: A Study*
Samuel P. Huntington's *The Clash of Civilizations and the Remaking of World Order*
Tony Judt's *Postwar: A History of Europe Since 1945*
David C. Kang's *China Rising: Peace, Power and Order in East Asia*
Paul Kennedy's *The Rise and Fall of Great Powers*
Robert Keohane's *After Hegemony*
Martin Luther King Jr.'s *Why We Can't Wait*
Henry Kissinger's *World Order: Reflections on the Character of Nations and the Course of History*
John Locke's *Two Treatises of Government*
Niccolò Machiavelli's *The Prince*
Thomas Robert Malthus's *An Essay on the Principle of Population*
Mahmood Mamdani's *Citizen and Subject: Contemporary Africa And The Legacy Of Late Colonialism*
Karl Marx's *Capital*
John Stuart Mill's *On Liberty*
John Stuart Mill's *Utilitarianism*
Hans Morgenthau's *Politics Among Nations*
Thomas Paine's *Common Sense*
Thomas Paine's *Rights of Man*
Thomas Piketty's *Capital in the Twenty-First Century*
Robert D. Putman's *Bowling Alone*
John Rawls's *Theory of Justice*
Jean-Jacques Rousseau's *The Social Contract*
Theda Skocpol's *States and Social Revolutions*
Adam Smith's *The Wealth of Nations*
Sun Tzu's *The Art of War*
Henry David Thoreau's *Civil Disobedience*
Thucydides's *The History of the Peloponnesian War*
Kenneth Waltz's *Theory of International Politics*
Max Weber's *Politics as a Vocation*
Odd Arne Westad's *The Global Cold War: Third World Interventions And The Making Of Our Times*

POSTCOLONIAL STUDIES

Roland Barthes's *Mythologies*
Frantz Fanon's *Black Skin, White Masks*
Homi K. Bhabha's *The Location of Culture*
Gustavo Gutiérrez's *A Theology of Liberation*
Edward Said's *Orientalism*
Gayatri Chakravorty Spivak's *Can the Subaltern Speak?*

PSYCHOLOGY

Gordon Allport's *The Nature of Prejudice*
Alan Baddeley & Graham Hitch's *Aggression: A Social Learning Analysis*
Albert Bandura's *Aggression: A Social Learning Analysis*
Leon Festinger's *A Theory of Cognitive Dissonance*
Sigmund Freud's *The Interpretation of Dreams*
Betty Friedan's *The Feminine Mystique*
Michael R. Gottfredson & Travis Hirschi's *A General Theory of Crime*
Eric Hoffer's *The True Believer: Thoughts on the Nature of Mass Movements*
William James's *Principles of Psychology*
Elizabeth Loftus's *Eyewitness Testimony*
A. H. Maslow's *A Theory of Human Motivation*
Stanley Milgram's *Obedience to Authority*
Steven Pinker's *The Better Angels of Our Nature*
Oliver Sacks's *The Man Who Mistook His Wife For a Hat*
Richard Thaler & Cass Sunstein's *Nudge: Improving Decisions About Health, Wealth and Happiness*
Amos Tversky's *Judgment under Uncertainty: Heuristics and Biases*
Philip Zimbardo's *The Lucifer Effect*

SCIENCE

Rachel Carson's *Silent Spring*
William Cronon's *Nature's Metropolis: Chicago And The Great West*
Alfred W. Crosby's *The Columbian Exchange*
Charles Darwin's *On the Origin of Species*
Richard Dawkin's *The Selfish Gene*
Thomas Kuhn's *The Structure of Scientific Revolutions*
Geoffrey Parker's *Global Crisis: War, Climate Change and Catastrophe in the Seventeenth Century*
Mathis Wackernagel & William Rees's *Our Ecological Footprint*

SOCIOLOGY

Michelle Alexander's *The New Jim Crow: Mass Incarceration in the Age of Colorblindness*
Gordon Allport's *The Nature of Prejudice*
Albert Bandura's *Aggression: A Social Learning Analysis*
Hanna Batatu's *The Old Social Classes And The Revolutionary Movements Of Iraq*
Ha-Joon Chang's *Kicking Away the Ladder*
W. E. B. Du Bois's *The Souls of Black Folk*
Émile Durkheim's *On Suicide*
Frantz Fanon's *Black Skin, White Masks*
Frantz Fanon's *The Wretched of the Earth*
Eric Foner's *Reconstruction: America's Unfinished Revolution, 1863-1877*
Eugene Genovese's *Roll, Jordan, Roll: The World the Slaves Made*
Jack Goldstone's *Revolution and Rebellion in the Early Modern World*
Antonio Gramsci's *The Prison Notebooks*
Richard Herrnstein & Charles A Murray's *The Bell Curve: Intelligence and Class Structure in American Life*
Eric Hoffer's *The True Believer: Thoughts on the Nature of Mass Movements*
Jane Jacobs's *The Death and Life of Great American Cities*
Robert Lucas's *Why Doesn't Capital Flow from Rich to Poor Countries?*
Jay Macleod's *Ain't No Makin' It: Aspirations and Attainment in a Low Income Neighborhood*
Elaine May's *Homeward Bound: American Families in the Cold War Era*
Douglas McGregor's *The Human Side of Enterprise*
C. Wright Mills's *The Sociological Imagination*

Thomas Piketty's *Capital in the Twenty-First Century*
Robert D. Putman's *Bowling Alone*
David Riesman's *The Lonely Crowd: A Study of the Changing American Character*
Edward Said's *Orientalism*
Joan Wallach Scott's *Gender and the Politics of History*
Theda Skocpol's *States and Social Revolutions*
Max Weber's *The Protestant Ethic and the Spirit of Capitalism*

THEOLOGY

Augustine's *Confessions*
Benedict's *Rule of St Benedict*
Gustavo Gutiérrez's *A Theology of Liberation*
Carole Hillenbrand's *The Crusades: Islamic Perspectives*
David Hume's *Dialogues Concerning Natural Religion*
Immanuel Kant's *Religion within the Boundaries of Mere Reason*
Ernst Kantorowicz's *The King's Two Bodies: A Study in Medieval Political Theology*
Søren Kierkegaard's *The Sickness Unto Death*
C. S. Lewis's *The Abolition of Man*
Saba Mahmood's *The Politics of Piety: The Islamic Revival and the Feminist Subject*
Baruch Spinoza's *Ethics*
Keith Thomas's *Religion and the Decline of Magic*

COMING SOON

Chris Argyris's *The Individual and the Organisation*
Seyla Benhabib's *The Rights of Others*
Walter Benjamin's *The Work Of Art in the Age of Mechanical Reproduction*
John Berger's *Ways of Seeing*
Pierre Bourdieu's *Outline of a Theory of Practice*
Mary Douglas's *Purity and Danger*
Roland Dworkin's *Taking Rights Seriously*
James G. March's *Exploration and Exploitation in Organisational Learning*
Ikujiro Nonaka's *A Dynamic Theory of Organizational Knowledge Creation*
Griselda Pollock's *Vision and Difference*
Amartya Sen's *Inequality Re-Examined*
Susan Sontag's *On Photography*
Yasser Tabbaa's *The Transformation of Islamic Art*
Ludwig von Mises's *Theory of Money and Credit*